Stuff It!

# Also by Lora Brody

Bread Machine Making—Perfect Every Time

Pizza, Focaccia, Flat and Filled Breads from Your Bread Machine: Perfect Every Time

Desserts from Your Bread Machine: Perfect Every Time

The Kitchen Survival Guide

The Entertaining Survival Guide

Broccoli by Brody

Cooking with Memories

Indulgences

Growing Up on the Chocolate Diet

Lora Brody Plugged In

Lora Brody and Max Brody

# Stuff It!

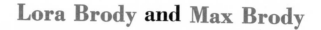

Fun Filled Foods to Savor and Satisfy

William Morrow and Company, Inc.
*New York*

Library of Congress Cataloging-in-Publication Data

Brody, Lora, 1945–
    Stuff it! / by Lora Brody and Max Brody.—1st ed.
        p.   cm.
    ISBN 0-688-15868-4
    1. Stuffed foods (Cookery)   I. Brody, Max, 1971–   .   II. Title.
TX836.B75   1998
641.8—dc21                                                        97-47320
                                                                      CIP

Printed in the United States of America

First Edition

1 2 3 4 5 6 7 8 9 10

BOOK DESIGN BY MADHOUSE STUDIOS

www.williammorrow.com

**Benjamin Jacob Brody—
born into the business—
this one's** for you.

# Contents

**Introduction**   **ix**

**Breakfast Stuff**   **1**

**Lunch Stuff**   **11**

**Appetizers**   **21**

**Pasta and Pizza and Calzones**   **45**

**Fish and Shellfish**   **59**

**Poultry and Meat**   **73**

**Vegetables**   **97**

**Chocolate- and Ice Cream–Stuffed Desserts**   **109**

**Fruit-Filled, Filled Fruit, and a Couple of Sweet Extras**   **125**

**Index**   **145**

# Introduction

**Lora:** Bridging the generation gap between me and my middle son, Max, are music (Bob Dylan, Elvis, The Beatles), the love of travel to exotic places, and food. Plus a certain kind of humor. During our cross-country tour of cooking schools in 1993, during which Max drove and prepped while I taught in small towns and large cities from Essex Junction, Vermont, to Nashville, Tennessee, we listened to hundreds of tapes, including one of George Carlin's classic monologues. Even though George Carlin is a product of my generation, it was Max who introduced me to his deliciously vulgar, nail-on-the-head brand of humor. It was the monologue about "stuff" that lit the fire that cooked up this book.

You may not quite follow the logic or sequence here, but trust me, everything in my life relates to food. And the leap from George Carlin saying, "There's all different ways of carrying your stuff," to a déjà vu of my mother sneaking last night's leftovers into tonight's main course makes perfect sense if you've grown up in the Brody family. "Hey, I've got a great idea for a book" didn't faze Max; after all, he's been hearing this all his life. The "Let's do it together!" part made him wince only slightly.

To his credit, Max tackled this project as he was completing the externship requirement for his degree at the Culinary Institute of America. His job as a line cook at Boston's venerable French restaurant Maison Robert left him little time for extracurricular activities.

His schedule meant we communicated mostly by Post-its. It was only by finding in the refrigerator unusual ingredients or dishes I hadn't made that I knew Max was holding up his end of the project. The times we did get to cook together were educational and fun. He showed me how to cook using every pot, pan, and utensil in the kitchen, and I taught him how to clean up to my satisfaction. Mostly we laughed, and in every instance we ate great food.

**Max:** Food and cooking have always brought our family together, whether it has been macaroni and cheese at the kitchen table, a picnic at the beach, Thanksgiving, or an eight-course meal at a French restaurant. That is why I don't find it a bit odd to be writing a book with my mother. Throughout my few years, my memories have been punctuated by meals with family and friends and the foods we have eaten. When I think of my fourth birthday, I remember the electric-blue Cookie Monster cake made for me and my classmates by good old Mom (almost as good as the cupcakes she made for me and the rest of my school on my sixteenth birthday). One of the few memories imprinted in my brain by the blur that was Paris is the dinner I had with my parents during which the waiter, with a truffle in one hand and a peeler in his other, slowly sliced slivers of heaven upon my risotto.

In a little town outside Bowling Green, Kentucky, during our cooking road-trip tour, my mother and I stopped in for breakfast at what appeared to be the only restaurant in town. After consulting the menu, each other, and the waitress, we agreed to have what turned out to be the worst peach cobbler we had ever eaten. Even though we found the food inedible, we still had a good laugh and a good meal; I have found that food (good or bad) is, like company, just a component of a memorable meal.

While writing this book, my mother and I had to test the recipes, giving us a great excuse to have friends over for dinner. Many nights would find us sitting around the dining-room table, a glass of wine in one hand and pen and paper in the other, jotting down notes and reminders and laughing and eating and living. So I hope, whether it's a simple snack for supper or an entree for eight, that the recipes in this book provide you and your guests and your family with many good meals and good times.

So, to begin. In the beginning there was wrapped food. We tried it, but, to tell you the truth, wrapped food reminds us of a pair of shoes that takes forever to lace up, hurts like hell to walk in, but looks so great and gets so many compliments that it's worth the trouble. There had to be an easier way—and there was. Meet the Birkenstocks of wrapped food: stuffed foods. The idea of presenting food in bundles is a terrific one, and clearly popular, since wrapped-food books are flying in and out of bookstores as fast as you can say "moo-shoo shrimp." However, all that prissy fussing and playing around could make you really crazy. Give us the faster and easier method, and let's get the food on the table, where it belongs.

 Stuffed food is downtown food. It's things like deviled eggs, celery sticks filled with whipped blue cheese, Cheddar-stuffed grilled burgers and calzones, stuffed peppers, chili-stuffed baked potatoes, and chocolate-ricotta–filled cannoli. It's homey, old-fashioned food that anyone can make. It's composed of things found in the supermarket (as opposed to the gourmet or super-natural grocery store). It's economical, made with inexpensive ingredients and leftovers. It's quick, it's adaptable (stuffings can be easily switched or substituted to accommodate special diets), and it's versatile (many dishes can be either appetizer or main course). Many of these recipes can be prepared ahead and refrigerated or frozen, to be cooked and served later. Stuffed foods can be baked, steamed, grilled, fried, microwaved, sautéed, or cooked in the pressure cooker or Crock-Pot, or over a campfire. These are dishes that little hands (with adult supervision, of course) could help make.

 Whether you are a rank novice or an experienced home cook, these recipes will speak to your desire to eat good food, made from good ingredients, and served up in a novel but unpretentious manner. Enjoy!

# Breakfast Stuff

# Sam's Best Breakfast

Makes **2** servings

**Lora:** *As the youngest member of this family, Sam is used to eating the tested recipes of the day for breakfast, lunch, and dinner. He's quite opinionated about which dishes go and which stay. He pronounced this easy-to-prepare croissant stuffed with scrambled eggs a "keeper" and advises "not to make it just for breakfast."*

**Max:** *Try adding sautéed onions and peppers to the eggs (although Sam, who never met a vegetable he liked, would never eat it this way).*

*This recipe makes enough for two servings, but it can easily be doubled or tripled.*

2 large, very fresh plain croissants (the taller they are, the prettier the final dish)

2 tablespoons butter

4 large eggs

1 tablespoon water

1 teaspoon salt

½ teaspoon freshly ground black pepper

Grated Parmesan or Cheddar cheese (optional)

Use a serrated knife to slice off the top quarter of the croissants. Set the tops aside. Use your fingers to pull out the soft insides of the croissants to form a pocket about 3 inches across and 2 inches deep.

Heat the butter in a small skillet over moderately high heat. While the butter is heating, use a whisk to mix the eggs, water, salt, and pepper together in a small mixing bowl. Beat for 30 seconds, then pour into the hot butter. Use a fork to move the eggs around in the skillet, scraping the bottom and sides often, until the eggs are softly scrambled. Just before the eggs are cooked, mix in the cheese, if you want it. Divide the eggs between the 2 croissants, spooning them carefully into the cavity and mounding them slightly. Cover with the tops and serve immediately.

# Diane Fitzgerald's Apple Pancake

**Makes 4 servings**

**Lora:** *Another of Sam's favorites. This omelet-shaped pancake is best described as a sweet, fruit-filled Yorkshire pudding. The pancake rises up during baking to form a bowl, which is then filled with sautéed apples. The recipe was generously shared by Diane Fitzgerald, who gets up early on Sunday mornings to make this special treat for her son, Dan, and his pal Sam Brody, who is a frequent weekend guest.*

**Max:** *Mom, how come you never get up early on Sunday mornings to make this for me?*

## For the pancake

3 large eggs
¾ cup milk
¾ cup unbleached all-purpose flour
1 teaspoon salt
1½ tablespoons unsalted butter
Confectioners' sugar

## For the filling

6 tablespoons (¾ stick) unsalted butter
3 large Granny Smith or Pippin apples, cored, peeled, and thinly sliced
¼ cup granulated sugar
½ teaspoon ground cinnamon
¼ teaspoon grated nutmeg

To make the pancake, preheat the oven to 450°F. In a medium-size mixing bowl, whisk together the eggs, milk, flour, and salt until very smooth. Melt the butter in a large, heavy ovenproof skillet over high heat. As soon as it sizzles, pour in the batter and immediately place in the oven. After 12 minutes, reduce the oven temperature to 350°F and bake another 10 minutes. The pancake will bubble and the edges will rise rather dramatically. Pierce the bubbles with the tip of a knife just to deflate. The pancake should be light brown and the edges crisp.

While the pancake is baking, prepare the apple filling. Melt the butter in another large skillet, then cook the apples over moderate heat, stirring, until tender but not mushy, 8 to 10 minutes, then add the sugar. Stir in the cinnamon and nutmeg. (The filling can be prepared ahead and reheated just before serving.)

When the pancake is ready, slide it onto an oval platter, pour the apple filling over one side, and fold the other side over. Sift some confectioners' sugar over the top. Serve it at once, slicing pieces off crosswise.

# Chocolate Chunk–Filled Scones

**Makes 12 scones**

**Max:** *Some might say we're pushing the definition of "stuffed" foods in this recipe. But these are so good I think the stretch is worth it. Think of it as a scone stuffed with chocolate chunks.*

**Lora:** *If you want to try something completely different, try adding either butterscotch morsels or peanut-butter chips to these scones for a teatime treat.*

2 cups unbleached all-purpose flour, measured after sifting

1 tablespoon baking powder

¾ teaspoon salt

¼ cup plus 2 tablespoons sugar, divided

10 ounces best-quality bittersweet chocolate, cut into ½-inch chunks

1¼ cups heavy cream

3 tablespoons butter, melted

Preheat the oven to 425°F with the rack set in the center position. The scones will bake on an ungreased heavy-duty baking sheet. Sift together the flour, baking powder, salt, and ¼ cup of the sugar into a 2-quart mixing bowl. Mix well with a fork to combine all the ingredients thoroughly. Mix in the chocolate, then add the cream, blending with the fork until the mixture holds together. The dough will be sticky.

Lightly sprinkle a clean work surface with flour and place the dough on it. Sprinkle the dough lightly with flour and knead it 10 times by pushing it down and away from you with the heel of your hand and folding it back over itself, giving it a quarter-turn each time. Pat the dough down into a 9-inch round. Flatten the top so it assumes a disk shape.

Brush the top with the melted butter, and then sprinkle with the remaining 2 tablespoons sugar. Use a long knife to cut the dough into 12 pie-shaped wedges and transfer the wedges to an ungreased heavy-duty baking sheet, leaving about 1½ inches between them. Bake until the tops are golden brown, 15 to 17 minutes. Serve warm or at room temperature.

# Stuffed Bran Muffins

**Makes 12 muffins**

**Lora:** *We're talking fiber here! Bran muffins stuffed with homemade stewed prunes make a nutritious breakfast or snack.*

**Max:** *My father finds these much better in the morning than a bowl of soggy bran flakes.*

## For the stewed prunes

12 pitted prunes
2 cups orange juice
1 lemon, cut in ½-inch-thick slices

## For the muffins

2 cups wheat or oat bran
2 cups whole-wheat pastry flour
(available at most whole-food
stores)
¾ cup raisins
1½ teaspoons baking soda
⅓ cup molasses
2 cups buttermilk

Place all the stewed-prune ingredients in a small saucepan over moderate heat. When the orange juice begins to simmer, reduce the heat to low, cover, and cook until the prunes are very soft but not falling apart, 15 to 20 minutes. Remove the pan from the heat and allow the prunes to cool in the liquid.

In a large mixing bowl, combine bran, flour, raisins, and baking soda. In a small mixing bowl, stir together the molasses and buttermilk, then pour it over the bran mixture. Let it stand for 20 minutes.

Lightly oil a 12-hole muffin tin. Preheat the oven to 350°F. Fill the muffin cups two-thirds full of batter. Remove the prunes one by one from the liquid and poke one into the batter for each muffin until the prune doesn't show. Bake until the muffins spring back slightly when pressed in the center about 30 minutes. Remove from the pan and allow to cool for 10 minutes on a wire rack; serve warm or at room temperature.

# Italian Toast

Makes 2 servings

**Max:** *Now for something entirely new and different for lunch or breakfast. This sausage-and-cheese–filled sandwich is cooked just like French toast, then topped with marinara sauce.*

**Lora:** *Try throwing a teaspoon or two of fresh herbs, such as thyme or oregano, into the egg mixture before dipping the bread. If you use a lean sausage, you might want to use a nonstick pan instead of adding additional oil to cook the toast.*

1 tablespoon olive oil
1 small onion, finely chopped
1 clove garlic, finely chopped
½ pound sausage, casing removed and meat crumbled
¼ teaspoon dried oregano
¼ teaspoon dried basil
1 cup marinara sauce
Four 1½-inch-thick slices challah or other rich egg bread
¾ cup whole-milk ricotta cheese (6 ounces)
1 large egg mixed with ¼ cup milk

Heat the olive oil in a large skillet set over moderate heat, then cook the onion, garlic, and sausage together, stirring, until the sausage is browned and crisp. Stir in the herbs. Reduce the heat to keep the skillet warm while you use a slotted spoon to remove the sausage to a small bowl, leaving the fat in the skillet. Heat the marinara sauce in a small saucepan over moderately low heat; keep warm. Spread 2 slices of the bread with a layer of ricotta and set aside briefly. Pour the egg-milk mixture into a flat-bottomed dish and dip 1 side of the 2 slices of bread that haven't been spread with ricotta in the mixture. Lay these 2 slices of bread in the hot skillet eggy side down and sprinkle with the cooked sausage. Dip the uncoated side of the bread slices spread with the ricotta in the egg mixture and lay it ricotta side down on top of the sausage to make a sandwich. Raise the heat under the skillet to moderate and cook until the bread is golden brown and crisp. Use a metal spatula to turn the sandwich over and cook on the other side until golden brown and crisp. To serve, place the toast on plates, dribble on a little marinara sauce, and serve immediately.

# Jumbo Lemon Cream–Filled Banana Oatmeal Muffins

**Makes 6 muffins**

**Lora:** *What to do with those overripe bananas no one wants to eat, plus that cup or so of cooked oatmeal left over from breakfast? Turn them into these super-delicious muffins loaded with flavor. No need to reach for the butter or cream cheese; the filling takes the place of a topping.*

**Max:** *I'll never look at overripe bananas quite the same way. When the kids are running out the door to school, hand them one of these—they are much easier to eat on the bus than a bowl of oatmeal.*

## For the stuffing

Two 3-ounce packages cream cheese, slightly softened

Grated rind of 1 lemon

1 tablespoon granulated sugar

## For the muffins

2 cups unbleached all-purpose flour, measured after sifting

1 teaspoon baking soda

½ teaspoon salt

½ teaspoon ground cinnamon

⅓ cup butter, softened

½ cup firmly packed dark-brown sugar

2 large or extra-large eggs

1 cup mashed very ripe bananas

½ cup cooked oatmeal

2 tablespoons fresh lemon juice

½ cup coarsely chopped pecans (optional)

Preheat the oven to 375°F with the rack set in the center position.

Generously butter a 6-cup jumbo-muffin tin or, if it is Teflon-coated, spray it with nonstick vegetable spray.

Either by hand or with an electric mixer, cream together the cream cheese, lemon rind, and granulated sugar until light and fluffy. Place this filling in the refrigerator while you make the muffin batter.

Sift the flour, baking soda, salt, and cinnamon together in a medium-size mixing bowl and set aside. In a large mixing bowl, either by hand or with an electric mixer, cream the butter and brown sugar together until light and fluffy. Add the eggs and beat to incorporate. Mix in the bananas, oatmeal, lemon juice, and pecans, if desired. Gently mix in the flour just until combined, taking care not to overbeat (which will make the muffins tough).

Spoon 2 generous tablespoons of the muffin mix into the bottom of each muffin cup and use a teaspoon to spread it around so it touches all the sides. Use 2 teaspoons to place a dollop of filling in the center of the batter. Spoon more batter over the filling to fill the cup two-thirds full, smoothing it to the edges to cover the filling.

Bake the muffins until the tops are deep golden brown, about 25 minutes. Cool in the pan for 5 minutes before turning out onto a wire rack. These are best right after baking, while they are still warm, but they're great at room temperature, too. They can be briefly rewarmed in the microwave.

# Lunch Stuff

# Ricotta-Stuffed Garlic Bread

**Makes 4 to 6 servings**

**Lora:** *This is more like an open-faced cheese sandwich masquerading as garlic bread. Make sure to enjoy it hot from the oven.*

**Max:** *I actually enjoyed the leftovers for breakfast the next day. I stuck it in the toaster oven for a few minutes to crisp it up.*

1 large loaf crusty Italian bread

1½ cups (10 ounces) ricotta cheese

1 teaspoon salt

½ teaspoon dried thyme

½ teaspoon dried oregano

½ teaspoon dried basil

6 cloves garlic, minced

2 tablespoons chopped fresh parsley leaves

6 tablespoons (¾ stick) butter, softened

¾ cup freshly grated Parmesan cheese

Preheat the oven to 350°F with the rack set in the upper third but not at the highest position.

Cut the loaf of bread in half lengthwise. Use your fingers to scoop out about half the soft bread to form a shallow cavity down the length of each half. Combine the ricotta, salt, and dried herbs and spoon this evenly into both cavities, spreading it smooth with a rubber scraper. Mix the garlic and parsley into the softened butter until well combined. Dot this mixture over the ricotta filling. Place the bread, filled side up, on a heavy-duty baking sheet. Sprinkle the Parmesan cheese over both halves and place the sheet in the preheated oven. Bake until the bread is toasted and the cheese is brown and bubbly, about 20 minutes. Serve by cutting with a serrated knife into generous slices.

# Stuffed Sourdough Reuben

makes **2**
large braids;

**4-6** servings

**Lora:** *This amazing recipe, which first appeared in my book* Pizza, Focaccia, Flat and Filled Breads, *was created by my pal P. J. Hamel of the* King Arthur Flour Baker's Catalogue. *Here's what she says about it: "You know how you order one of those overstuffed reuben sandwiches, and when you take your first bite the sauerkraut slides out one end of the bread and the corned beef and Swiss shoot out the other? Well, this braided sandwich roll, which conveniently encases the filling within secure boundaries of bread, will solve your slippery reuben problem forever." Making sourdough bread becomes a snap when you use my Sourdough Bread Enhancer (available from the* King Arthur Flour Baker's Catalogue, *800-827-6836.*

**Max:** *Sauerkraut is definitely an acquired taste. Try making this with coleslaw if you're not enamored with sauerkraut.*

## For the bread

1 tablespoon active dry yeast

1 cup unbleached all-purpose white flour

2 cups white (or light) rye flour

1½ teaspoons sugar

1½ teaspoons salt

1½ cups water, or more as needed

3 tablespoons vegetable oil

1½ teaspoons caraway seeds

2 tablespoons Lora Brody's Sourdough Bread Enhancer

## For the filling

2 tablespoons prepared mustard of your choice

½ pound thinly sliced corned beef

One 16-ounce can sauerkraut, well drained

½ pound thinly sliced Swiss cheese

For the food processor: Place the yeast, flours, sugar, and salt in the work bowl of a processor fitted with the plastic blade. With the machine running, add the oil and enough water through the feed tube so the dough forms a smooth, soft ball. Process for another 40 seconds after the water is absorbed. Allow the dough to rest for 10 minutes with the cover on, then process another 40 seconds, adding the caraway seeds during the very last few seconds. With the cover on the machine, allow the dough to rise until doubled in bulk.

For the stand mixer: Place the yeast, flours, sugar, salt, and caraway seeds in the mixing bowl of a stand mixer fitted with the dough hook. With the mixer on the lowest speed, add the oil and water enough to form a slack, moist ball of dough. This will take 5 to 6 minutes. Don't be tempted to add flour so that a discrete ball forms, since this will make the bread dry. Knead on medium speed for 10 minutes, then cover and let rest for 20 minutes. On medium speed, knead again until the dough is soft and supple, another 7 to 8 minutes. Cover the bowl and allow the dough to rise in a warm place until doubled in bulk.

For the bread machine: Place all of the ingredients in the machine, program the machine for Dough, and press Start. Check the dough midway through the second kneading cycle; it should have formed a smooth, pliable ball. If it's stiff and gnarled, add more water; if it hasn't formed a discrete ball, add more flour.

No matter what method you have used, punch down the dough and divide it in half. Roll each half out to a 12-by-15-inch rectangle. Transfer each rectangle to a lightly greased 13-by-18-inch heavy-duty baking sheet.

Work with one piece of dough at a time. Starting with a short end of the dough, make 7 slits from the edge of the dough toward the center, 1½ inches apart, each 5 inches long. Do the same with the other short end of the dough. You'll now have a solid center piece of dough 5 by 12 inches, and flanking strips of dough; the effect is somewhat like an insect with eight pairs of legs.

For the filling: Fill the solid, center piece of dough by spreading it with 1 tablespoon of the mustard, then layering on half the corned beef, half the sauerkraut, and half the cheese. Crisscross the strips of dough over the filling, anchoring the strips opposite their side of origin. Tuck the two ends of the braid underneath. Repeat the entire process with the remaining piece of dough.

Tent the braids with lightly greased plastic wrap and let them rise for 1 hour. Preheat the oven to 375°F. Bake the braids until they're golden brown and the filling is starting to sizzle, 25 to 30 minutes. Remove the braids from the oven and let cool for 10 minutes before cutting.

# Salsa-Stuffed Subs

**Makes 3 twelve-inch or 4 eight-inch subs**

*Lora: Each of these large subs will feed two people, and a small one should satisfy a starving person. For instant gratification, we've used store-bought bread dough in this recipe. You can use your own favorite homemade white bread dough, if you wish.*

*Max: Substitute prosciutto, Brie, and sun-dried tomatoes for the salsa and you will have a delicious "uptown" sub.*

1½ pounds white bread dough (defrosted, if store-bought)

## For the stuffing

One 16-ounce container fresh salsa (the kind that comes from the refrigerated case of the market), as spicy you wish

¾ to 1 cup grated Cheddar or jack cheese, to your taste

Allow the dough to rest on a lightly floured work surface for 10 minutes before beginning. Lightly spray a heavy-duty baking sheet or baguette pan with nonstick vegetable spray. Place the salsa in a fine-mesh strainer and press out any watery liquid. Divide the dough into three or four equal pieces. Gently roll and shape the dough into either three 12-inch loaves or four 8-inch loaves and place them in the prepared pan. If you are using a baking sheet, place them 2 inches apart.

Use your fingers to scoop out bread and create a narrow trough about 2 inches deep down the center of each loaf from end to end. Use a spoon or your fingers to place the drained salsa in the trough, mounding it slightly. Sprinkle the cheese on top and allow the loaves to rise, uncovered, in a warm place until almost doubled in bulk, 30 to 50 minutes.

Preheat the oven to 400°F with the rack set in the center position. Bake the subs until the crusts are brown and the cheese has melted, about 25 minutes. Allow the subs to cool for 10 minutes before serving. Serve hot, warm, or at room temperature.

# Greek Salad in Pita Pockets

**Makes 2 sandwiches**

**Lora:** *Usually Greek salad is served with wedges of pita bread. Here the salad comes inside the bread.*

**Max:** *You can also use soft lavash to make rolled sandwiches with this filling. If you're taking it for lunch, make sure to wrap it in plastic wrap to prevent leaks.*

2 small pitas (regular or whole-wheat)

3 cups loosely packed fresh spinach leaves, stems removed, well washed, dried, and large leaves torn in half

1 small red onion, thinly sliced

1 cup crumbled feta cheese

1 ripe plum tomato, thinly sliced

½ cup pitted sliced black olives (the dry oil-cured are best)

¼ cup extra-virgin olive oil

2 tablespoons red-wine vinegar

Use a sharp knife to slice a 6-inch-long opening on the edge of each pita. This should allow you to separate the sides of the bread to create a pocket. Combine the spinach, onion, feta, tomato, and olives in a large mixing bowl. Add the oil and vinegar and toss to mix. Stuff the salad into the pitas and serve immediately.

# Phyllo Stuffed Spinach Pie

**Makes 10**
**first-course or**
**6 to 8**
**main-course**
**servings**

**Max:** *This is an adaptation of the traditional Greek dish spanakopitas, which are individual triangles of phyllo stuffed with spinach and feta cheese. The pie is simple to make, but if you haven't worked with phyllo before, it will probably take some practice until you are up to speed. Since this is a rustic dish, looks aren't everything.*

**Lora:** *A good trick for working with phyllo dough is to prepare all the other ingredients before opening the phyllo package, and then to keep a damp dish towel over the dough to prevent it from drying out.*

## For the stuffing

Two 10-ounce packages frozen
　　chopped spinach, defrosted
2 tablespoons vegetable or olive oil
1 large Spanish onion, chopped
8 ounces feta cheese, crumbled
½ cup finely chopped fresh dill
2 large eggs, lightly beaten
½ cup pine nuts (optional), toasted
　　(see Note, page 49)

## For the pie

¼ cup (½ stick) butter
¼ cup vegetable oil
5 sheets frozen phyllo dough,
　　defrosted

Place the spinach in a fine-mesh strainer and use your hands or a spoon to press out as much liquid as possible. Heat the oil in a medium-size skillet and cook the onion, stirring occasionally, until slightly browned and very soft. In a large mixing bowl, stir together the spinach, onion, feta, dill, eggs, and pine nuts, if desired. Don't overmix—the ingredients should retain their integrity.

To make the pie, place the butter and oil in a small saucepan, bring to a simmer, then cool slightly. Brush a 10- or 11-inch pie pan generously with the butter/oil mixture. Lay a sheet of phyllo in the pan with the edges overlapping the rim. Brush the phyllo with some of the butter mixture; don't worry about coating every bit and don't worry if the phyllo rips or breaks. Lay a second piece of phyllo over the first, but rotate it slightly so the overlapping edges don't line up with those of the first sheet. Coat with the butter mixture. Cover with a third sheet, rotating it slightly as well. Continue in this manner until all the sheets are used. Brush the final sheet with the butter mixture, then add the filling, spreading it so it is evenly distributed in the pan. Fold the phyllo leaves, one at a time, over the filling, brushing the top of each with the butter mixture as you put it in place. When the pie is completely covered, brush the top with the remaining butter mixture.

The pie can be frozen at this point (for up to 3 months) wrapped tightly in plastic wrap (defrost for 30 minutes at room temperature before baking) or baked immediately.

To bake, preheat the oven to 425°F with the rack set in the center position. Bake the pie until the top is deep golden brown and the bottom of the pie can be loosened from the pan, about 25 minutes. Serve hot, warm, or at room temperature, cutting into wedges.

# Appetizers

# Bread Bowl in Honor of Jim Dodge

**Makes 6 to 8 appetizer servings**

*When our friend the world-renowned pastry chef and teacher Jim Dodge comes to dinner, we try to come up with something creative. This appetizer—easy to prepare, but stunning to look at—was inspired one July afternoon. Jim pronounced it "fine indeed." The recipe calls for eggplant dip (sometimes called Poor Man's Caviar), but you can use any Middle Eastern–type prepared salad or dip except hummus, which would be too runny. Though this can be eaten with a fork, we found it easier to eat pizza-style—with your hand.*

1 large round loaf of white Italian-style bread, about 12 inches in diameter and 4 to 6 inches high in the center

2 cups Poor Man's Caviar, home-made (recipe follows), or store-bought eggplant dip

4 ounces feta cheese (1 cup crumbled)

3 tablespoons olive oil

Preheat the broiler to high with the rack set in the upper third of the oven. Use a serrated knife to slice off the top third of the loaf and use your fingers to pull out the soft insides, leaving at least a 1-inch shell and reserving the insides. Place the loaf on an ovenproof baking sheet. Pour and scrape the dip into the cavity. In a food processor or blender, grind 1½ cups of the reserved bread insides to crumbs with the cheese (the easiest way to do this is to add the pieces of bread and cheese through the feed tube or top while the machine is on). Mound the crumbs on top of the dip, overlapping about 1 inch onto the bread. Push gently to pack the crumbs down. Drizzle the top with the olive oil and broil until the topping is deep golden brown (the color will not be uniform), 4 to 6 minutes. Allow the loaf to remain at room temperature for at least 2 hours or as long as 4 hours before cutting into slices to serve. This dish is better if it's not refrigerated.

# Poor Man's Caviar

Makes about 8 appetizer servings

2 small eggplants, about 1 pound total, cut in half lengthwise

2 large red bell peppers, cut in half and seeded

1 medium-size red onion, cut in ½-inch-thick slices

½ to ⅔ cup olive oil

2 cloves garlic, very finely minced

2 small stalks celery, minced

2 tablespoons tomato paste

1 cup chopped peeled tomatoes

1 tablespoon sugar

3 tablespoons capers, drained

½ cup minced fresh parsley leaves

¼ cup balsamic or red-wine vinegar

Salt to taste

Preheat the broiler to high with the rack set in the upper third of the oven. Prick the skin of the eggplants with a fork or sharp paring knife. Place the peppers on a work surface and flatten them with your hand. Coat the eggplants, peppers, and onion well with some of the olive oil. Broil until the onion and the skins of the eggplants and peppers are slightly charred, about 5 minutes per side. Remove the onions and eggplant and continue cooking the peppers until the skins bubble and turn black. Drop the peppers into a paper bag and, when cool, slip off the skins.

In a small skillet, heat the remaining olive oil over medium heat, then cook the garlic until soft and translucent but not brown, stirring.

Chop the eggplants, onion, and peppers until coarse. Mix in the garlic, then the rest of the ingredients, and chill well before serving. Serve with triangles of pita bread.

# Classic Deviled Eggs

**Makes** 12

**Lora:** *It wouldn't be a real picnic without deviled eggs. Just be sure to keep them well chilled if your picnic is far from home.*

**Max:** *What about putting a little pesto and some chopped prosciutto in the filling? You'll have Green Eggs and Ham!*

**Lora:** *Max . . .*

6 extra-large eggs
1 tablespoon white vinegar
2 teaspoons Dijon mustard
4 or 5 drops Tabasco sauce, to your taste
1 tablespoon snipped fresh chives
Salt and freshly ground black pepper to taste
¼ cup mayonnaise
Paprika for garnish

Place the eggs in a medium-size saucepan, cover with cold water, and add the vinegar. Place the pan, uncovered, over medium-high heat and bring to a boil. Reduce the heat to a simmer and cook for 15 minutes. Drain, rinse under cold water until cool enough to handle, and peel. Refrigerate until totally cooled, then use a sharp knife to slice the eggs in half lengthwise and carefully scoop out the yolks. Place the yolks in a bowl and mash with a fork. Add mustard, Tabasco, and chives and season with salt and pepper. Stir in the mayonnaise.

Use a small spoon or a pastry bag fitted with a star tip to fill each egg white with about 2 teaspoons of the egg-yolk mixture and dust the top with paprika. Refrigerate until ready to serve.

# Anchovy-Stuffed Olives

**Makes** 12      *Wow! For all you salt lovers out there—here's the ultimate snack.*

12 very large pitted green olives (you may have to get them with the pimentos—if so, pull them out and discard)

6 large anchovy fillets, drained and cut in half crosswise.

Slice each olive from top to bottom, but not all the way through, to make a trough. Roll or fold the anchovy as small as possible and stick it into the olive. Have water handy for quenching your salt-induced thirst.

# Stuffed Snow Peas

Makes 8 servings

*These delicate appetizers are a bit tedious to make, but they're easy, and very popular at parties, so put on the music, grab a stool, and get to work.*

1 quart water

32 large snow peas

1¼ cups low-fat ricotta cheese

1 tablespoon dillweed

2 cloves garlic, finely minced

3 tablespoons grated Parmesan cheese

32 cooked small-to-medium-size shrimp, shelled and deveined

32 sprigs fresh dill, each 1 inch long

In a large stockpot, bring the water to a boil. Blanch the snow peas by dropping them in the boiling water and cooking until they turn bright green, about 30 seconds. Rinse them in very cold water to stop the cooking. Cut the stem ends off the snow peas and use a small, sharp knife to slit them open along one edge.

In a small bowl, mix together ricotta, dillweed, garlic, and Parmesan. Open the slit side of each snow pea and fill the cavity with the ricotta mixture.

Garnish each stuffed snow pea with a shrimp and a tiny sprig of dill. Serve chilled.

# Sun-dried Tomatoes Stuffed with Tapanade and Parmesan

**Makes 6 to 8 servings**

**Max:** *As soon as this book was done, Mom was out the door on her way to Italy. I got to go back to another world-class destination: Hyde Park, New York.*

**Lora:** *Hey, I brought you back porcini mushrooms and truffle oil! I also brought back the recipe for these lovely cocktail tidbits. I saw them in a street market in Soragna, in the heart of Emilia-Romagna—the place where Parmigiano-Reggiano cheese is produced.*

24 large oil-packed sun-dried tomato halves, drained, 3 to 4 tablespoons of the oil reserved

24 oil-cured black olives, pitted

24 large green olives, pitted

⅓ cup capers, drained

2 large cloves garlic, finely minced

½ teaspoon dried thyme, or 2 teaspoons chopped fresh thyme leaves

½ cup freshly grated Parmesan cheese

Blot any excess oil from the tomatoes with paper towels and lay them, cut side up, on a serving dish. Either in a food processor or by hand, chop the olives into coarse pieces. Mix in the capers, garlic, thyme, reserved oil, and cheese. Spread a layer of the stuffing on top of each tomato and serve at room temperature with lots of napkins, for these tend to be on the oily side.

# Sam Arnold's Jalapeños Stuffed with **Peanut Butter**

**Makes** 10 **servings**

**Lora:** *Max and I are proud to be AFMs—that's Arnold Family Members. Anyone who has had the great treat of eating at the Fort in Morrison, Colorado, knows firsthand the warmth and creative genius of this master of Old West cookery. The following very unusual appetizer will liven up not only your mouth, but conversation as well. As Sam says, "Pop the entire pepper into your mouth so you're not left with a mouthful of hot jalapeño and not enough peanut butter" to quell the fire. If you nibble, you squeeze out the peanut butter, change the ratio, and make it "very hot indeed."*

*Sam says the very best canned jalapeño peppers are the kind pickled in vinegar and vegetable and sesame oils, with bay leaves, sliced onions, and carrots, as opposed to the kind pickled simply in vinegar; they're available in Spanish or Latin American groceries, and gourmet shops.*

**Max:** *Be sure to have a beer in the other hand.*

One 12-ounce can pickled jalapeño peppers, drained
1½ cups best-quality peanut butter (chunky or smooth)

Slice the pickled jalapeños in half lengthwise not quite all the way through, leaving the 2 halves attached at the stem end. Use a small, sharp knife or spoon to remove the seeds and ribs under running water. It's best to wear a pair of rubber gloves to protect your hands while you do this—those seeds are *hot*. Pack the halves with peanut butter, press together, and arrange on a serving plate.

**Variation** Sam also suggests mixing a little Major Grey's chutney in with the peanut butter for a "nice fruit sweetness that also buffers the burn."

# Stuffed Brie

Makes 12 to 16 servings

*Lora: Here's a novel cold-weather appetizer that's a snap to prepare, and will make your guests happy they came to your house to eat. This works best with a slightly underripe Brie, which means firm to the touch. You might ask someone from the cheese department at your market to help you select a suitable one.*

*Max: If you're going to serve this warm, make sure to use plates: it takes on a volcanic personality, with the Brie flowing like lava.*

One 9-inch wheel of Brie, slightly underripe, well chilled
1 cup pecan halves
¼ cup firmly packed dark-brown sugar

Remove the plastic wrap from the Brie, turn it over, and remove the foil label if there is one. Do not remove the white rind from the brie. Dip a very sharp, thin knife in boiling water and slice the Brie cleanly in half horizontally, so you have two rounds. To do this, you will have to remove the knife, rinse it clean, and dip it in boiling water several more times to cut through the Brie completely. Separate the halves. Place the pecans in one layer over the surface of one of the cut sides. Sprinkle on the brown sugar, then replace the top of the Brie cut side down to make a "sandwich." Cover the Brie tightly in plastic wrap and refrigerate until 1 or 2 hours before you are ready to serve. Allow the cheese to come to room temperature. Some of the brown sugar will have leaked out the sides; you can wipe it away or leave it, as you wish. Cut the cheese into wedges and serve on plates with thinly sliced pumpernickel bread.

**Variation** The Brie can also be served warm, which makes it much more like fondue and a tad messier to eat, although no less delicious. Place the Brie on a rimmed (this is very important) ovenproof serving dish. A ceramic quiche dish works great. Cover loosely with a sheet of aluminum foil and place on the middle rack of a preheated 325°F oven for 10 to 15 minutes, depending on how runny you want the cheese. Serve by scooping up with crackers, or place a wedge on top of a plate of mixed greens.

# Buffalo Thighs

Makes 4 servings

**Max:** *This appetizer chicken dish was inspired by buffalo wings, which actually should be called "Buffalo wings," since they come from the city, not the animal. Here the chicken is wrapped around the blue cheese, then breaded and baked. These are great both hot and at room temperature. I've even enjoyed them straight from the fridge for breakfast (don't tell Mom).*

4 cups cornflakes

1 pound boneless, skinless chicken thighs

6 ounces blue cheese, cut into rough chunks (⅓ cup)

1 large egg mixed with ¼ cup milk

2 tablespoons butter, plus more for greasing the baking dish

Preheat the oven to 375°F with the rack set in the center position. Butter an 8-by-10-inch ovenproof baking dish. Place the cornflakes in a heavy-duty plastic bag and use a rolling pin to crush them into coarse crumbs. Lay the chicken between 2 pieces of plastic wrap and use the rolling pin to roll and pound each piece into a thin, flat cutlet; don't get carried away or the chicken will disintegrate. Lay a generous piece of blue cheese in the center of each chicken thigh and lift up the sides to cover it. Use your hands to press the chicken gently into a rough ball and dip it in the egg mixture, then place it in the bag with the cornflakes and coat well by pressing the crumbs into the surface of the chicken. Lay the chicken in the prepared dish and dot each with a small piece of the butter. Bake until a cake tester inserted in the center comes out hot, about 25 minutes. Serve hot, warm, or cold.

# Louise Goldsmith's Famous Knishes

**Makes 8 servings**

**Lora:** *Appetizer, lunch, brunch, or just when you're in the mood, there's nothing like a homemade knish! We've given you the choice of three different fillings.*

**Max:** *And if you're a really good Jewish mother, you'll make them all!*

## For the dough
3¼ cups unbleached all-purpose flour

1 teaspoon salt

1 cup (2 sticks) cold butter, cut into ½ tablespoons

1 cup water

## For potato filling
3 tablespoons butter

1 large onion, chopped

2 large Idaho potatoes, peeled and sliced

1 teaspoon salt

1 teaspoon freshly ground black pepper

½ cup heavy cream or milk

## For cabbage filling
3 tablespoons olive or vegetable oil

1 large onion, chopped

2 cups shredded green cabbage

1 tablespoon caraway seeds

## For kasha filling
3 tablespoons vegetable oil

1 large onion, chopped

1 cup coarse kasha (buckwheat groats)

1 large egg, slightly beaten

To make the dough, mix the flour and salt together on a work surface, then make a mound with a well in the center. Add the butter and use your fingers to rub it into the flour until it forms coarse crumbs. Dribble in the water slowly and knead briefly to make a ball of dough. Cover the dough with plastic wrap and refrigerate for at least 2 hours.

To make the potato filling, melt the butter in a skillet over moderate heat, then cook the onion, stirring, until golden brown. Place the sliced potatoes in a medium-size saucepan and cover with water. Bring to a boil, then reduce the heat to a simmer and cook until fork tender, 15 to 20 minutes. Drain well and add the onion along with any liquid left in the skillet, and remaining potato-filling ingredients. Mash by hand until lump-free. Cool to room temperature before forming the knishes.

To make the cabbage filling, melt the oil in a medium-size skillet over moderate heat, then cook the onion, stirring, until golden brown. Add the cabbage and continue cooking until it is very limp. Stir in the caraway seeds. Cool to room temperature before using.

To make the kasha filling, heat the oil in a large skillet over moderate heat, then cook the onion, stirring, until golden brown. Remove from the heat and add the kasha and egg, mixing to moisten all the grains. Return to mod-

2 cups chicken, vegetable, or beef
    broth, heated to a simmer
3 tablespoons butter or margarine
1 teaspoon salt
Freshly ground black pepper to
    taste

## To complete

1 large egg mixed with 1 table-
    spoon water

erate heat and stir constantly until the egg has dried (you'll see the egg white). Add the hot broth, butter or margarine, and salt and season with pepper. Cover the skillet, reduce the heat to a simmer, and cook for 15 minutes. Fluff the grains with a fork. If they are still quite moist, cover and cook an additional 5 minutes. Allow to cool before using.

Preheat the oven to 400°F with the rack set in the center position. Line a heavy-duty baking sheet with parchment paper or aluminum foil. Apply a light coating of nonstick vegetable spray.

Divide the knish dough into 4 equal pieces and, working with 1 piece at a time, roll it out into an 8-by-10-inch rectangle on a lightly floured work surface. Using a fourth of the filling of your choice, form a row with it on the edge closest to you. Moisten the farthest edge. Roll the dough to form a tight cylinder, with the seam side down. Use a sharp knife to score the dough at 1-inch intervals. Repeat with the other pieces of dough, placing the rolls on the baking sheet at least 2 inches apart. Brush the tops of the rolls with the egg wash and bake until the rolls are deep golden brown, 15 to 17 minutes. Remove from the oven and slice where the rolls are scored. Serve hot, warm, or at room temperature.

These freeze beautifully; wait until they're completely cooled, then freeze in a single layer on a baking sheet. When they're completely frozen, place in heavy-duty zippered-top plastic bags for up to 6 months. Defrost, covered, then reheat in a preheated 350°F oven for 10 to 12 minutes.

# Mozzarella en Carrozza

**Max:** *This recipe, which translates from the Italian into "Mozzarella in a Carriage," is the ultimate toasted-cheese sandwich. Serve it hot with the tangy caper, lemon, and anchovy sauce as a first course before a light dinner, since it's pretty filling. The preparation can be completed up to the frying step as much as six hours ahead. Refrigerate the carrozzas until ready to cook. Prepare the simple sauce just before you cook the carrozzas.*

**Lora:** *I was really looking forward to eating these in Italy, but was disappointed to see that over there they were just like greasy grilled-cheese sandwiches. This homemade version is so much better.*

## For the sauce

½ cup (1 stick) butter
¼ cup olive oil
8 flat anchovy fillets
2 tablespoons capers, drained
Juice of 1 large lemon
1 cup packed fresh Italian parsley leaves, chopped

## For the carrozzas

1 wide loaf Italian bread
4 very thin slices prosciutto or smoked turkey
8 ounces fresh whole-milk mozzarella cheese, cut into 4 equal slices
¼ cup milk
2 large eggs
Vegetable oil for deep-frying

Heat the butter and olive oil together in a skillet. When melted, add the anchovies and stir constantly over moderate heat until they dissolve. Stir in the remaining sauce ingredients and cook to heat thoroughly, another 2 or 3 minutes. Keep at room temperature until ready to use.

Cut the bread into 8 equal slices and trim off the crusts. Grind the crusts and any remaining bread in a food processor or blender to make coarse crumbs. Use your hands to flatten the slices of bread slightly. Wrap a slice of prosciutto or turkey around each slice of mozzarella and place on a slice of bread. Top with the other slice to make a small sandwich. Pinch the edges together. Stir the milk together with the egg, then dip the sandwich briefly in the mixture without allowing it to get soggy. Roll the sandwich in the bread crumbs, then dip in the milk/egg mixture one more time. Use your fingers to seal the seams. Heat 2 inches of oil in a deep skillet set over high heat to 375°F and fry the carrozzas 2 at a time (or 1 at a time) until very deep golden brown. To serve, place a carrozza on a small plate and top with sauce. Serve hot.

# Millie's Pierogi

Makes 6 servings

*Here's Grandma Millie's famous dumpling recipe. Get the sour cream and butter ready.*

## For the dough

2 cups unbleached all-purpose flour

½ teaspoon salt

2 large eggs

½ cup water

## For the filling

2 tablespoons vegetable oil

1 medium-size onion, finely diced

2 cloves garlic, minced

1 pound ground lean beef, or 1 pound chicken livers, trimmed of membranes, rinsed, and dried

1 hard-boiled egg, peeled and cut into pieces

1 teaspoon salt

Freshly ground black pepper to taste

## To cook and serve

2 tablespoons salt

Melted butter

Sour cream

To make the dough, place the flour in a mound on your work surface and sprinkle the salt over it. Make a well in the center of the mound and add the eggs, working them into the flour with your fingers. Add the water and continue kneading until the dough is firm, adding a bit more water if necessary to allow the dough to form a ball. Cover and let rest for 10 minutes at room temperature.

To make the filling, heat the oil in a skillet over moderate heat, then cook the onion, stirring, until golden brown. Add the garlic and cook another 2 to 3 minutes. Add the beef or livers and cook, stirring frequently, until well browned. Remove from the heat. Add the egg and chop the mixture either by hand or in a food processor until finely chopped but not puréed. Season with salt and pepper. Set aside.

Roll the dough into a long coil about 1 inch in diameter and cut it into ¼-inch pieces. Roll each piece into a small ball, then, on a lightly floured work surface, roll each ball out into a thin circle about 2½ inches in diameter. Place a teaspoon of the filling in the center of each circle, moisten the outside edge of the dough with water, and fold it over to form a crescent. Seal the edges with the tines of a fork.

Bring a large pot of water to a rapid boil and add the 2 teaspoons salt. Drop the pierogi 8 at a time into the boiling water and cook until the dough is cooked through, 3 to 5 minutes. Remove with a slotted spoon, drain briefly, and serve with melted butter and sour cream.

# Asian Pork Pot Stickers

Makes 36

**Max:** *This recipe can just as easily be prepared with chicken or shellfish. Try using thinly sliced snow peas, bean sprouts, and rock shrimp. You can make a vegetarian version by leaving out the meat and substituting small cubes of soft tofu.*

**Lora:** *Store-bought wonton wrappers can be found in the refrigerated section of your supermarket.*

### For the filling
1 cup finely chopped cooked pork tenderloin

⅓ cup finely chopped bok-choy leaves and stems or cabbage

⅓ cup finely chopped celery

¼ cup finely chopped scallions, green and white parts

1 tablespoon soy sauce

1 tablespoon dry sherry

1 teaspoon cooking oil of your choice

1½ teaspoons cornstarch

### To make the pot stickers
About 36 wonton wrappers

6 tablespoons cooking oil of your choice

1 cup water

Chinese mustard

Soy sauce

To make the filling, in a mixing bowl combine the pork, bok choy, celery, and scallions. Combine the soy sauce, sherry, and oil; stir in the cornstarch until dissolved. Pour the soy mixture over the pork mixture and toss to coat. Cover and chill for 30 minutes.

Cut the wonton wrappers into 4-inch circles with a cookie cutter. (Keep the wrappers covered with a damp cloth when not working with them.) Spoon about 2 teaspoons of the filling in the center of each round. Bring up the sides and seal the edges with water. Transfer to a baking sheet and cover with a dry clean kitchen cloth. Repeat with the remaining rounds and filling.

In a large skillet, heat 2 tablespoons of the oil. Carefully place half the pot stickers in the skillet (do not let the sides of the pot stickers touch). Cook over medium heat till the bottoms are browned, about 1 minute. Carefully add ½ cup of the water to the skillet. Reduce the heat to medium-low, cover, and simmer for 10 minutes. Uncover and cook until the water evaporates, 3 to 5 minutes. Add more oil, if necessary. Cook, uncovered, for 1 minute. Transfer the cooked pot stickers to a baking sheet and place in a preheated 250°F oven to keep warm. Repeat the procedure with the remaining pot stickers, oil, and water. Serve with Chinese mustard and soy sauce.

# Max's Spring Rolls

Makes 12

**Max:** *Spring rolls are fun to make and so much better than the kind you get in most restaurants. As with the pot stickers, you can turn these into a vegetarian appetizer by leaving out the chicken and substituting small cubes of soft tofu.*

## For the filling

1 pound ground chicken

¼ pound finely sliced Napa cabbage

1 tablespoon peeled and minced fresh ginger root

½ cup finely sliced scallions, white and green parts

3 tablespoons soy sauce

3 tablespoons mild toasted sesame oil

1 large egg

## For the rolls

12 large wonton wrappers

2 tablespoons all-purpose flour

3 tablespoons water

Peanut oil for frying

Quick Dipping Sauce (recipe follows)

In a large mixing bowl, combine all the filling ingredients. Place 1½ to 2 tablespoons of the mixture in the center of each wonton wrapper. In a small mixing bowl, combine the flour with the water until it makes a sticky paste. Coat the edges of each wrapper with the flour paste, then fold two of the sides toward the center and roll the wrapper into a cylinder.

In a wok or a deep skillet or sauté pan, heat 2 inches of peanut oil. Keep the temperature of the oil at about 375°F over a medium-high flame. When the oil is hot enough, carefully place the spring rolls several at a time in the wok and fry until golden brown, turning to cook all sides. Drain on paper towels and serve hot with the dipping sauce.

## Quick Dipping Sauce

¼ cup soy sauce

1½ tablespoons white vinegar

1½ tablespoons mild toasted sesame oil

1 scallion, minced

1 large clove garlic, minced

4 to 6 drops Tabasco sauce, to your taste

1 tablespoon sugar

Place all the ingredients in a small mixing bowl and whisk to blend.

# Mock Maki

**Lora:** *Now that sushi is as ubiquitous as hot dogs, everyone wants to try his or her hand at making it at home. If you're not into seaweed and raw fish, this Americanized version of sushi rolls will appeal to you.*

**Max:** *Since I'm definitely into raw fish, I suggest making this with thin slices of the very freshest raw salmon. Shop at a top-quality fish market when buying ingredients for sushi, and make sure your fish man knows you are buying the fish to eat raw.*

¼ cup mayonnaise

1 teaspoon Tabasco sauce

2 teaspoons soy sauce

1 tablespoon tomato paste

Four 10-inch flour tortillas

1 cup ½-inch pieces cooked scallops, shrimp, crabmeat, or lobster meat, or any combination of the above

1 ripe avocado, peeled, pitted, and cut into 8 slices

1 scallion, cut into 4 pieces

Mix together the mayonnaise, Tabasco sauce, soy sauce, and tomato paste. Spread the tortillas with the mixture. Sprinkle the shellfish pieces over the sauce. Place 2 slices of avocado down the middle of each tortilla and place a scallion piece over the avocado. Roll the tortilla into a tight cylinder, moistening the outside edge with water to seal the roll. Cut the roll on the diagonal into 8 pieces. Repeat with the remaining ingredients. Serve the maki with a small dipping dish of soy sauce.

# Niçoise Roll-ups

Makes 4
sandwiches or
32 appetizers

**Max:** *This Mediterranean-style tuna appetizer is so wonderfully tasty no one would dream it took you only minutes to make. You have the option of using the entire roll as a sandwich, or cutting it into slices to serve with drinks or as a snack.*

**Lora:** *Using imported tuna packed in olive oil is a key in getting the authentic taste.*

One 7-ounce can Italian-style tuna in olive oil
1 tablespoon capers, drained
½ cup black olives, drained, pitted, and sliced
¼ cup packed fresh Italian parsley leaves
2 flat anchovy fillets (optional)
Four 10-inch flour tortillas
4 very thin slices Bermuda onion
1 cup shredded mozzarella cheese

Place the tuna and its oil, the capers, olives, parsley, and anchovies in the work bowl of a food processor and process just until blended but not puréed.

Spread this mixture over the surface of the tortillas. Top each with a slice of onion and an equal amount of the cheese. Roll into a tight cylinder, moistening the outside edge with water to seal. Eat as a roll-up sandwich or slice each roll on the diagonal into 8 pieces to serve as a pick-up snack.

# Scallop Roll-ups

**Makes about 24**

*If you are looking for an elegant but easy cocktail tidbit, then look no further. It takes but a minute to fix these pretty little packages, and just a few more minutes to cook them. Buy the large sea scallops (as opposed to the smaller bay scallops).*

1 pound sea scallops, rinsed, muscle removed

¼ pound very thinly sliced prosciutto

Preheat the oven to 425°F with the rack set in the upper third. Select an ovenproof baking dish large enough to hold all the scallops in one layer. Divide each slice of prosciutto in half or thirds and wrap each scallop snugly with a piece. Lay the scallops, seam side down, in the baking dish and cook until the scallops are cooked all the way through, about 8 minutes. Serve hot, or warm, passed with toothpicks.

# Smoked Turkey and Muenster
# Roll-ups

Makes about 48

**Lora:** *Here's a do-ahead passed pick-up appetizer that you can serve with drinks. It also makes great picnic fare.*

**Max:** *I vote for making these with really sharp Cheddar and substituting Dijon mustard for the chutney.*

Four 3-ounce packages cream cheese, softened

¼ cup mango chutney

3 tablespoons finely chopped fresh dill

8 flat (8-to-9-inch) whole-wheat mountain breads or other flatbreads, such as lavash

1 bunch watercress, coarse stems removed, washed and dried

1 pound very thinly sliced Muenster or Swiss cheese

1 pound very thinly sliced smoked turkey

1 large sweet onion (optional), very thinly sliced and separated into rings

In the food processor or blender or by hand, mix the cream cheese with the chutney and dill until smooth. Spread a thin layer of this mixture over each bread. Cover with some watercress, then a slice of Muenster or Swiss. The cheese should cover about two thirds of each bread, with ⅓ inch of the rim left uncovered.

Spread over this another thin layer of the cream-cheese mixture and more watercress, then add a slice of turkey over the watercress. Once again, spread on the cream-cheese mixture and add the remaining watercress and turkey, and the onion rings.

Roll the breads up tightly, starting from the filled edge. Slice each roll-up diagonally into 6 or 7 pinwheels about ¾ inch wide. Discard the trimmed edges. Run a toothpick through each slice and place slices on a platter in a spiral pattern.

# Chicken Empanadas

**Makes** 10 **servings**

*These savory turnovers can be made ahead of time and frozen, uncooked, until you're ready to pop them in the oven. You can cook them frozen.*

## For the dough

1½ cups unbleached all-purpose flour

1½ teaspoons salt

1¼ cups (2¼ sticks) cold butter, cut into pieces

⅔ cup solid vegetable shortening (Crisco)

3 large eggs plus 3 large egg yolks

¼ cup hot water

## For the filling

2 whole boneless, skinless chicken breasts, chopped

½ cup firmly packed dark-brown sugar

¼ cup chopped fresh coriander (cilantro) leaves

1½ tablespoons paprika

1 medium-size onion, diced

1 cup bottled barbecue sauce

1 teaspoon salt (omit if the barbecue sauce is very salty)

## To assemble

¼ cup whole milk

Green Chile Salsa (recipe follows)

To make the dough, place the flour and salt in the work bowl of a food processor fitted with the plastic blade or a stand mixer fitted with the flat paddle. Add the butter and shortening all at once and pulse, or mix on low speed, until the mixture resembles coarse crumbs. Add the whole eggs, yolks, and hot water and process or mix on medium speed until the mixture forms a smooth ball. Cover tightly with plastic wrap and set aside at room temperature.

Combine all the filling ingredients in a medium-size mixing bowl.

Preheat the oven to 400°F with the rack set in the center position. Line a heavy-duty baking sheet with aluminum foil.

Place the dough on a lightly floured surface and form it into a ball. Cut the ball in half and roll out each half into a cylinder. Cut the dough into 1-inch segments and roll these into balls. Flatten each ball with your hand and roll it out with a rolling pin to ¼-inch thickness.

Place 2 tablespoons of the filling in the center of each round of dough, wet the edges of the dough with a little water, and fold them over to close. Crimp the edges with the tines of a fork and place the empanadas on the prepared baking sheet. Brush the tops with milk and bake until golden brown, about 20 minutes. Serve with the salsa.

# Green Chile Salsa

2 tablespoons olive or vegetable oil

3 green chiles, chopped

½ cup chopped fresh coriander (cilantro) leaves

4 scallions, white and green parts, finely sliced

1 clove garlic, minced

½ tablespoon chopped fresh oregano leaves

Heat the oil in a medium skillet over high heat. Add the remaining ingredients and cook, stirring constantly, for 3 minutes. Remove to a food processor or blender and process until the mixture is still a bit chunky. Serve warm or at room temperature.

# Pasta and Pizza and Calzones

# Quick Manicotti Stuffed with
## Spinach, Pesto, and Ricotta

**Makes** 4 **servings**

**Max:** *We decided it was time for Dad to try his hand at stuffing something. We gave him the ingredients for this recipe and told him to get creative.*

**Lora:** *David turns out to be the Michelangelo of Manicotti. No one would ever know this was made with egg-roll wrappers instead of pasta.*

12 cups fresh spinach leaves, stems removed, rinsed very well or one 10-ounce package frozen chopped spinach, defrosted, liquid pressed out

½ cup water (optional)

3½ cups ricotta cheese (whole- or skim-milk)

½ cup prepared pesto

½ cup pine nuts (optional), toasted (see Note, page 49)

Salt and freshly ground black pepper

8 large egg-roll wrappers (6½ inches square)

2 tablespoons butter, melted

½ cup freshly grated Parmesan cheese

Preheat the oven to 350°F with the rack set in the upper third but not in the highest position. Lightly butter a 9-by-15-inch baking dish.

If using fresh spinach, place it in a large saucepan with the water. Cover and steam over medium heat just until wilted, 3 to 4 minutes, then immediately drain, press out any excess water, and chop into medium-size pieces. In a large mixing bowl, combine the spinach, ricotta, pesto, and pine nuts (if desired), and season with salt and pepper.

Place the egg-roll wrappers on a work surface and place a generous ⅓ cup of the filling in middle of each wrapper, leaving ½ inch on each side and 2 inches on both the top and the bottom. Fold down the top of the wrapper and bring up the bottom to form a soft roll. Place the rolls in the prepared baking dish seam side down, drizzle with the melted butter, and sprinkle generously with the grated cheese. Cover the dish with a sheet of aluminum foil and bake for 15 minutes, covered, then remove the foil and bake until the tops are light golden brown and the filling is bubbling, another 15 minutes. Serve by placing 2 manicotti on each plate. Pass additional grated cheese.

# Jumbo Shells Stuffed with Feta and Dill in Fresh Tomato Sauce

**Makes 6** main-course or

**8** first-course servings

**Max:** *Jumbo shell noodles make a terrific container for any number of fillings. The following version is perfect for summer. For wintertime, the sausage stuffing on page 100 also works well.*

**Lora:** *Take care not to overcook the shells, since they tend to fall apart.*

12 ounces jumbo shell noodles

### For the filling

2 tablespoons olive oil

2 shallots, minced

¾ pound feta cheese

1 pound ricotta cheese

⅓ cup freshly grated Parmesan cheese

Finely grated zest and juice of 1 lemon

¼ cup chopped fresh dill or 1 tablespoon dillweed

1 teaspoon freshly ground black pepper

½ cup pine nuts, toasted (see Note)

### For the sauce

8 to 10 ripe plum tomatoes, or 4 large ripe tomatoes, sliced (skins on, seeds removed if you wish)

½ cup olive oil

2 tablespoons balsamic vinegar

1 tablespoon sugar

1 teaspoon salt

Bring a large pot of water to a rapid boil. Add the shells, stir gently, and when the water returns to the boil, reduce the heat to a gentle simmer and cook until the noodles are al dente, 9 or 10 minutes.

Meanwhile, prepare the filling and sauce. Heat the oil in a small skillet and cook the shallots, stirring, until lightly browned. In a large mixing bowl, or in the work bowl of a food processor fitted with the metal blade, place the shallots, cheeses, lemon zest and juice, dill, and pepper and mix or process until smooth. Stir in the pine nuts by hand.

Pour the cooked shells into a colander to drain well. When cool enough to handle, fill each shell with about a tablespoon of the filling. Some of the shells will break or crack—usually they can be pushed back together once the filling is added, since it will hold them together. Place the filled shells close together in a single layer in a large baking dish. Prepare the sauce while the oven is preheating to 350°F with the rack set in the center position.

Place all the sauce ingredients in the food processor and pulse only until coarsely chopped. Spoon the sauce over the shells, cover with a sheet of aluminum foil, and bake for 30 minutes, removing the foil during the last 5 minutes of baking. Serve hot.

**Note:** To toast pine nuts, preheat the oven to 350°F with the rack set in the upper third but not the highest position. Place the nuts in a single layer on a heavy-duty baking sheet and roast for 10 minutes, then reverse the pan, back to front, and roast another 5 to 10 minutes, occasionally shaking the pan or stirring with a wooden spoon, to rotate the nuts. Cook until golden brown.

# Fresh Ravioli with Two Stuffings

Makes 4 to 6 servings

**Max:** *The pasta dough in this recipe can be made by hand or in a food processor, or frozen pasta sheets may be found at your supermarket. If you are using frozen pasta sheets, let the dough thaw completely before using.*

**Lora:** *It was fun to watch Max make these (pasta's not my forte, so I've never attempted ravioli). It was much easier than I had imagined.*

## For the dough

2 cups all-purpose flour

2 large eggs plus 1 large egg yolk

3 tablespoons water

## For the spinach and ricotta filling

3 tablespoons olive oil

3 cloves garlic, finely minced

8 ounces fresh spinach leaves, stems removed, well rinsed, shaken dry, and coarsely chopped

¼ teaspoon salt

¼ teaspoon freshly ground black pepper

8 ounces ricotta cheese

## For the sun-dried tomato and goat cheese filling

⅓ cup oil-packed sun-dried tomatoes, drained

¾ cup (6 ounces) goat cheese

6 fresh basil leaves, roughly chopped

To make the dough by hand, place the flour in a mound on a clean, dry work surface. Lightly beat the whole eggs and egg yolk together. Make a well in the middle of the flour and pour in the beaten eggs. Fold the eggs into the flour and keep mixing until incorporated. If the dough is dry and crumbly, add some of the water, and sprinkle flour on the work surface to keep the dough from sticking. If the dough is wet and sticky, add more flour in small amounts. Knead the dough until it is smooth and elastic. Put the dough aside to rest, covered with a damp kitchen cloth, for ½ hour.

To make the dough in a food processor, insert the plastic blade. Place the flour, beaten eggs, and water in the work bowl. Pulse the ingredients together until smooth and elastic. If the dough is dry and crumbly, you may need to add some more water; if it is sticky and wet, add more flour in small amounts. Cover the dough with a damp kitchen cloth for ½ hour to rest.

To make the spinach and ricotta filling, heat the oil in a large skillet over moderate heat. Add the garlic and cook, stirring frequently, until the garlic is light golden brown, 2 to 3 minutes. Add the spinach and cook, stirring frequently,

**To cook and serve**
12 cups water
2 tablespoons salt
Butter
Freshly grated Parmesan cheese

just until it wilts but does not give up its liquid. Add the salt and pepper. In a large mixing bowl, combine the ricotta and spinach. Let the mixture cool and set aside.

To make the sun-dried tomato and goat cheese filling, in a food processor or by hand blend all the ingredients together until smooth.

To roll out the dough, have the egg wash and pastry brush handy. Sprinkle a light coating of flour on a clean, dry work surface and place the dough in the center. With a rolling pin, roll the dough out into an 18-inch square ⅛ inch thick. It is important that the dough and work surface remain well floured so the dough doesn't stick.

Use a ruler to cut the dough into 81 squares by marking nine 2-inch squares down the length and width of the dough. Place a tablespoon of the filling in the center of half (40) of the squares. Then brush the egg wash along the edges of the dough. Cover with a second square and seal the edges by lightly pressing with your fingers, then crimp with a fork, making sure that all the sides are sealed. You will have 1 square left over.

At this point the ravioli can be frozen for up to 3 months to be used in the future, or it can be cooked immediately. To cook the ravioli, bring the water to a rapid boil. Add the salt. Add the ravioli, and when the water returns to a boil, reduce to a simmer, stirring gently once or twice to separate the ravioli, until fork tender, about 15 minutes. Drain, and serve immediately with butter and freshly grated Parmesan cheese.

# Deep-dish Stuffed Pizza

**Makes 8 servings**

**Lora:** *It's easy and surprisingly quick to make your own pizza dough, or you can use defrosted store-bought white bread dough.*

**Max:** *This is a vegetarian recipe. For you meat eaters out there, feel free to add thin slices of prosciutto, cooked crumbled sausage, sliced meatballs, or sautéed ground turkey.*

## For the herb crust

1 tablespoon dry yeast

3½ cups all-purpose flour

2 teaspoons salt

3 tablespoons Lora Brody's Dough Relaxer (optional for an easier-to-roll crust)

1 teaspoon dried basil

½ teaspoon dried oregano

1 teaspoon dried parsley

1¼ cups water

⅓ cup olive oil

## For the filling

8 ounces thinly sliced turkey breast (smoked turkey breast is also delicious)

8 ounces roasted red peppers, split open so they lie flat

8 ounces smoked mozzarella cheese, cut into ½-inch-thick slices

½ teaspoon dried basil

½ teaspoon dried oregano

1 teaspoon freshly ground black pepper

Olive oil for brushing the pizza

To prepare the crust in a food processor

Place the dry ingredients and herbs in the work bowl of a food processor fitted with the plastic blade. With the machine running, add the water and oil and process for 40 seconds after they are absorbed. The dough should be extremely wet and may not even form a ball. Allow it to rest for 10 minutes, then process another 40 seconds. With the cover on the machine, allow the dough to rise until doubled in bulk.

To prepare in a stand mixer

Place all the dry ingredients and herbs in the mixing bowl of a stand mixer fitted with the dough hook. With the mixer on lowest speed, add the water and oil. The dough should be very wet. Knead on medium speed for 10 minutes, cover, and let rest for 20 minutes, then knead until the dough is soft and supple but still on the wet side, another 7 to 8 minutes. Cover the bowl and allow the dough to rise in a warm place until doubled in bulk.

To prepare in a bread machine

Place all the ingredients in the machine, program for Dough, and press Start. The dough should form a smooth, firm ball after the first few minutes of kneading.

At the end of the rise, no matter the method, remove to a lightly oiled work surface. Cover with a clean kitchen cloth and allow to rest while you assemble the filling.

This pizza goes into a cold oven, so there is no preheating. Oil or spray a 12-inch spring-form pan or a deep-dish pizza pan with nonstick vegetable spray. Divide the dough into 2 pieces, then roll the first out into a 14-inch circle and lay it in the bottom of the prepared pan. It will shrink slightly, so push the dough out from the center to the edges so that the edges touch the rim of the pan as much as possible.

Leaving a 1-inch border around the edge, lay the turkey over the dough, then the red peppers, and finally the cheese. Sprinkle with the dried herbs and pepper. (The cheese and turkey are salty, so additional salt is not necessary.) Moisten the edge of the dough with a little water, then roll out the second piece of dough to a 14-inch circle. Lay the second circle over the filling, pushing the edge of the dough down firmly to seal the 2 layers. Brush the top with olive oil and place the pizza on the center shelf of a cold oven. Set the thermostat for 450°F and bake the pizza until the top is a deep golden brown, about 30 minutes.

Allow the pizza to cool for 10 minutes in the pan before releasing the springform or cutting. Serve hot, warm, or at room temperature.

# Zucchini, Summer Squash, and Vidalia Onion–Stuffed Calzones

**Makes 4 servings**

**Lora:** *Vidalia onions, sweet enough to eat raw, are shipped from the South during the spring months. If you have a hankering for this bountiful garden pizza but cannot get Vidalias, use Spanish onions instead. Again, this recipe calls for store-bought dough; feel free to use your own favorite white-bread or pizza-dough recipe.*

**Max:** *Roasted garlic cloves give the calzones a nice nutty taste.*

## For the filling

- ½ cup corn oil, divided
- 1 pound Vidalia onions, thinly sliced
- 1 head roasted garlic (see Note), cooking oil reserved
- 2 cloves garlic, minced
- 1 pound zucchini, scrubbed and thinly sliced
- 1 pound summer squash, scrubbed and thinly sliced
- Salt and freshly ground black pepper
- 4 ripe plum tomatoes, cut into 1-inch-thick slices

## To assemble the calzones

- ⅓ cup cornmeal
- Reserved garlic cooking oil

## For the dough

- 1 pound white-bread or pizza dough, at room temperature

In a large skillet over moderate heat, heat ¼ cup of the oil, add the garlic and cook for 2 minutes, then add the zucchini and summer squash, stirring frequently until tender. Remove the cooked vegetables to a large mixing bowl, then, without washing the skillet, heat the remaining ¼ cup oil and cook the onions until light golden brown. Combine the vegetables and roasted garlic and season with salt and pepper, then strain the mixture, reserving the liquid.

Preheat the oven to 400°F with the rack set in the center position. Lightly dust 2 heavy-duty baking sheets with the cornmeal and set them aside. Place the dough on a lightly floured work surface, cover with a clean kitchen cloth, and let rest for 5 minutes. Divide the dough in half, and roll each half out into a 12- or 14-inch circle. Transfer one circle to the prepared baking sheet, and spoon half the squash mixture over half the circle, leaving a ¼-inch border of uncovered dough along the edge. Place half the sliced tomatoes over the onion squash mixture. Brush some of the reserved vegetable liquid around the perimeter of the dough and fold the dough over to form a plump half-moon. Use the tines of a fork to seal the edges, then brush the reserved garlic oil over the surface of the dough and with a pair of scissors cut three 1-inch-long vents in the top. Repeat with the other piece of dough and the rest of the filling. Bake until golden brown, about 25 minutes.

Serve hot, warm, or at room temperature.

**Note:** To roast garlic, preheat the oven to 300°F, with the rack set in the center position. Select a large, firm head of garlic. Remove any loose dry skin. Place the garlic in a small (2-cup) oven-proof ramekin or small ovenproof dish large enough to hold the entire head and with sides at least as high as the garlic. Add ½ cup olive oil, cover tightly with foil, and bake for 1 hour, or until the garlic is very soft. Cool covered, then use your hands to squeeze out the garlic pulp. Reserve the oil.

# Calscones

*What do you get when you cross a calzone with a scone? A calscone, of course. Diane Crane, the heart, soul, and brains behind Titterington's Old English Bake Shop, Ltd., in Woburn, Massachusetts, came up with this novel idea for a savory filled scone. Here's the recipe. If you are craving other flavors of great scones, you can order them from Diane by calling 800-670-9959.*

## For the filling

⅓ cup ricotta cheese

⅓ cup grated Monterey Jack cheese

½ cup frozen chopped spinach, thawed and drained

⅓ cup diced roasted red peppers

1 large egg beaten with 2 tablespoons milk

½ teaspoon salt

¼ teaspoon freshly ground black pepper

## For the scones

3 cups unbleached all-purpose flour

3 teaspoons baking powder

½ teaspoon salt

¼ teaspoon dried basil

¼ teaspoon dried oregano

¼ teaspoon freshly ground black pepper

1 clove garlic; minced

⅔ cup grated Parmesan cheese

9 tablespoons unsalted butter, softened

½ cup whole milk

2 large eggs

## To assemble

1 large egg mixed with 2 tablespoons milk or heavy cream

Combine all the filling ingredients in a medium-size mixing bowl and stir to blend completely.

For the scones, mix together the dry ingredients, the seasonings, garlic, and Parmesan in a large mixing bowl. Use 2 knives in a crisscross motion to cut the butter into the flour until it resembles coarse crumbs. Add the milk and eggs only to wet the dry ingredients. Turn the mixture onto a lightly floured work surface and gently knead until the mixture holds together enough to form a ball. Don't overknead: this will make the scones tough.

To assemble, preheat the oven to 375°F with the rack set in the center position. Select a heavy-duty baking sheet (but don't grease it). Roll the dough out to a ¼-inch thickness, then use a 2½- or 3-inch round cookie cutter or glass to cut out 12 to 14 circles. Any used dough can be rerolled and cut. Place half the circles on the baking sheet 1 inch apart. Use your finger to make a shallow impression in the center of each. Add 1 tablespoon of the filling. Brush the egg wash around the filling, then top with another circle, gently pressing the edges together to seal in the filling. Brush the tops with the wash and bake until golden brown, 16 to 20 minutes. Cool for 10 minutes on a wire rack, then enjoy warm, if possible. Scones are best eaten the day they are made—and not refrigerated.

# Jumbo Shells Stuffed with Kasha

**Makes 6** main-course or **8** side-dish servings

*This is a take on the traditional Jewish recipe kasha varnishkas, which are bow-tie noodles tossed with buckwheat groats. Here the grains are stuffed into pasta shells.*

## For the filling

3 tablespoons vegetable oil

1 large onion, chopped

2 cloves garlic, minced

1 cup coarse kasha (buckwheat groats)

1 large egg, slightly beaten

2 cups chicken, vegetable, or beef broth, heated to a simmer

3 tablespoons butter or margarine

1 teaspoon salt

Freshly ground black pepper to taste

5 or 6 drops Tabasco sauce, to your taste

½ cup grated Swiss cheese

## To complete

12 ounces jumbo shells, cooked according to package directions and drained

½ cup (1 stick) butter, melted

1 cup dried bread crumbs

½ cup grated Parmesan cheese

Additional melted butter or sour cream (optional)

To make the filling, heat the oil in a large skillet over moderate heat, then cook the onion, stirring, until golden brown. Add the garlic and cook, stirring, an additional 2 minutes. Remove from the heat and add the kasha and egg, mixing to moisten all the grains. Return to moderate heat and stir constantly until the egg has dried (you'll see the egg white). Add the hot broth, butter or margarine, salt, and pepper, cover the skillet, reduce the heat to a simmer, and cook for 15 minutes. Fluff the grains with a fork. If they are still quite moist, cover, and cook an additional 5 minutes. At the end of the cooking time, stir in the Tabasco and Swiss cheese.

Preheat the oven to 350°F with the rack set in the center position. Lightly spray a large baking dish with nonstick vegetable spray. When the shells are cool enough to handle, fill each one with a generous amount of the kasha mixture, fold them closed, and place seam side up in the baking dish. Mix together the melted butter, bread crumbs, and Parmesan and sprinkle over the shells. Cover with a sheet of aluminum foil and bake for 20 minutes, then remove the foil and bake an additional 5 minutes. Serve hot, drizzled with additional melted butter or a dollop of sour cream, if desired.

# Fish and Shellfish

# Little Fish, Big Fish

**Makes 6 servings**

*Those tiny goldfish-shaped crackers make a delicious breading for lots of dishes, but we thought some sort of fish fillet was the most appropriate. Here flounder (or sole) is wrapped around a shrimp-and-rice stuffing, rolled in crumbs and baked.*

2 cups Cheddar-cheese Goldfish crackers (4 ounces)

2 tablespoons butter

1 medium-size onion, finely chopped

1½ cups cooked rice

4 ounces cooked shrimp, cut into small pieces

⅓ cup grated Cheddar cheese (2 ounces)

1 teaspoon dillweed

1 large egg

Six 5-to-6-ounce white-fish fillets (such as flounder or sole)

1 large egg mixed with 3 tablespoons milk

2 tablespoons butter, melted

Preheat the oven to 350°F with the rack set in the center position. Butter an 8- or 9-inch baking dish. Pulverize the Goldfish, either in a food processor or by placing them in a plastic bag and crushing with a rolling pin. Set aside.

Heat the butter in a small skillet over moderate heat, then cook the onion, stirring, until translucent. In a large mixing bowl combine the cooked onion and any cooking liquid, the rice, shrimp, cheese, dillweed, and egg and mix gently but thoroughly.

Lay the fillets out on the work surface. Take 2 tablespoons of the stuffing at a time and use your hands to fashion it into a ball. Place a filling ball in the center of each fillet and close the ends of the fillet around it, making a compact roll. Secure with a toothpick, then dip in the egg/milk mixture. Some of the filling may fall out—just poke it back in. Roll the fish in the cracker crumbs to coat generously, then set the rolls in the prepared dish. Drizzle with the melted butter and bake, uncovered, until the fish flakes and is no longer translucent and a cake tester inserted in the center comes out hot, about 20 minutes. Remove the toothpicks and serve immediately.

# Big Fish, Little Fish

Makes 4 servings

**Lora:** *Anchovies are an acquired taste, cultivated by people who, in our book, know what's good. Some people just can't figure out what all the hoopla is about. This recipe is for those who worship the tiny salty tidbits and the magic they work on food. Trout fillets are stuffed with a parsley-based pesto-type mixture, breaded, and panfried.*

**Max:** *Pass the beer. Lots of it.*

### For the stuffing

1 cup loosely packed fresh curly parsley leaves

One 2-ounce can anchovy fillets and their oil

Zest and juice of 1 large lemon

1 tablespoon capers, drained

2 tablespoons garlic oil or olive oil

### To complete

4 trout (6 to 8 ounces each), boned, butterflied with heads on, rinsed and patted dry

1 large egg mixed with 2 tablespoons milk

1 cup plain dry bread crumbs

### To panfry

¼ cup (½ stick) butter

1 tablespoon vegetable oil

½ cup dry white wine

¼ cup chopped fresh Italian parsley leaves

Place all the stuffing ingredients in the work bowl of a food processor fitted with the metal blade or a blender. Process, using the pulse button, or blend until the mixture has formed a rough paste

Lay the trout open, skin side down, on the work surface. Spread ¼ of the filling over each of the fillets so that it covers the inside area. Close the fish (this will be a little more challenging to do now that the fish is stuffed) and press gently down to "seal." If it doesn't close, try spreading the stuffing into the head and tail, or removing a little of it.

Pour the milk/egg mixture into a shallow pan, and the bread crumbs into another. Dip the fish in the egg/milk mixture, then lay it in the crumbs. Turn the fish over to coat the other side. Repeat until all the fish are coated. At this point the fish can be refrigerated for up to 4 hours before proceeding.

In a large skillet over medium heat, melt the butter with the oil, and when it is sizzling, add the trout. It's better not to crowd the fish (they'll end up steaming instead of frying), so, if your skillet isn't large enough, do it in 2 batches or use 2 skillets. Cook the fish until the flesh flakes, 4 to 5 minutes, then use 2 forks to turn the fish carefully to the other side. Cook another 4 to 5 minutes; the skin should be crisp and the flesh should flake easily. Place the trout on a serving plate, or on individual dinner plates. Add the wine and chopped parsley to the skillet and cook for 2 to 3 minutes, scraping up the browned bits from the bottom of the skillet. Pour over the fish and serve immediately.

# Baked Fish Stuffed in Lettuce

Makes **6** servings

**Max:** *You can use pretty much any white fish fillet here; my choice, if you can get some, would be striped bass, since it has more personality than flounder or sole.*

**Lora:** *Red snapper would also be great.*

⅓ cup balsamic vinegar

4 large shallots, minced

2 cloves garlic, minced

1 tablespoon vegetable oil

6 large Boston-lettuce leaves, taken from the outside of the head

6 white-fish fillets

2 teaspoons dried thyme

1 teaspoon dried tarragon

2 tablespoons olive oil

In a small saucepan over moderate heat, place the vinegar, shallots, and garlic and cook until softened, about 5 minutes. Preheat the oven to 350°F with the rack set in the upper third but not at the highest position. Use the vegetable oil to coat a large baking sheet lightly. Place the lettuce leaves on the baking sheet; do not let them overlap.

Wash and pat dry the fillets, then sprinkle them with thyme, tarragon, and 1 tablespoon of the olive oil. Spread the fillets evenly with the shallot mixture. Starting with the small end of each fillet, roll it up and over the filling and place the roll on top of a lettuce leaf. Fold the lettuce around the fish and place the packet seam side down on the baking sheet. Brush the packets with the remaining tablespoon oil. Cover the baking sheet with a sheet of aluminum foil and bake until a small, sharp knife inserted in the center of the packet comes out hot, 20 to 30 minutes. Remove the foil and serve hot.

# Salmon Chowder in a Bread Bowl

**Makes 6 servings**

**Max:** *When we were children, my brother Jon and I always got a kick out of eating bread-bowl soups. Our mother would usually make them on the coldest nights in winter, and we would stuff ourselves silly.*

**Lora:** *Except back then I used canned salmon.*

6 round domed bread loaves, at least 8" in diameter

3 tablespoons butter

4 shallots, minced

1 teaspoon dried tarragon

4 medium-size red potatoes, left unpeeled, thinly sliced

2 teaspoons Worcestershire sauce

½ teaspoon salt

⅛ teaspoon ground white pepper

2 cups fish stock (available in the frozen-food section of the supermarket) or canned vegetable broth

1½ pounds salmon steaks, ¾ to 1 inch thick

1 lemon, thinly sliced

1 bay leaf

1 cup dry white wine

1 cup heavy cream

6 strips bacon, cooked until crisp and broken in small pieces, for garnish

Use a serrated knife to slice off the top third of each loaf of bread. Use your fingers to scoop out the interior to form a bowl, leaving a 1½-inch thickness of bread inside. Save the crumbs for another use. In a large skillet over moderate heat, melt the butter; add the shallots and cook, stirring, until softened but not browned. Add the tarragon, potatoes, Worcestershire sauce, salt, pepper, and fish stock. Reduce the heat to moderately low, cover the skillet, and simmer gently for 15 minutes.

Add the salmon steaks to the skillet in a single layer; cover with the lemon slices, then add the bay leaf. Pour in the wine. Cover and cook over low heat until the salmon flakes when tested with a fork and the potatoes are tender, 10 to 12 minutes. Remove and discard the bay leaf and lemon slices. Remove the salmon steaks to a plate; pick out the bones, remove the skin, and cut the salmon into 1½-inch chunks. Stir the cream into the skillet and cook over moderate heat until the mixture simmers. Cook for 5 more minutes, then gently mix in the salmon. Taste and add more salt if needed. Place the bread bowls in rimmed dishes or large bowls, spoon the chowder into the bread bowls, garnish with the bacon, and serve immediately.

# Fourth of July Stuffed Salmon to Feed a Crowd

**Makes 10 to 12 servings**

**Lora:** *The New England tradition of serving salmon and peas makes us happy to see the Fourth of July roll around every year. Last year we tried stuffing large sides of salmon with wild rice and crabmeat. It was such a success that we may never go back to the poached version. This dish is great served either hot or cold. You can even cook it in the barbecue!*

**Max:** *I think my parents are relieved that these days I'm more interested in cooking than in trying to blow my hands off with firecrackers.*

## For the stuffing

1½ cups cooked wild rice

1 generous cup crabmeat
(6 ounces), picked over for
cartilage and shells

1 medium-size onion, chopped
and cooked, stirring, in
2 tablespoons butter until
light golden brown

2 tablespoons fresh lemon juice

¼ cup chopped fresh dill, or
1 tablespoon dillweed

¼ cup mayonnaise

## To prepare

2 whole salmon fillets (2 to
2½ pounds each), skin on

½ cup (1 stick) butter, melted

½ cup dry white wine

Gently mix together the stuffing ingredients in a large mixing bowl and set aside.

Use a pair of tweezers to remove any remaining pin bones running down the center of the fillets. Lay a 24-inch piece of double-thickness cheesecloth in a roasting pan large enough to hold the salmon, allowing the ends to overlap the sides of the pan. Brush with the butter an area of the cheesecloth in the bottom of the pan the approximate size of the salmon. Lay one fillet in the pan. Mound the filling down the center of the fillet, making it higher in the center than at the edges. Top with the second fillet. Brush the top of the fish with more butter, then fold the cheesecloth over the top of the fillet, tucking the ends securely under the fish to make a compact bundle. Brush the top of the cheesecloth with the remaining butter and pour the wine into the bottom of the roasting pan. At this point the fish can be refrigerated for up to 6 hours.

To cook, preheat the oven to 350°F with the rack set in the upper but not highest position of the oven. If you have an ovenproof meat thermometer, insert it into the fish so that the end rests in the stuffing. You can also use an instant-read thermometer to check for doneness. Bake the fish for 40 minutes, then check the internal temperature. Continue cooking fish, checking every 10 minutes, until it reaches the desired temperature, 135° to 140°F.

To barbecue, preheat the grill to 350°F to 400°F. Make sure the baking pan does not cover the entire surface of the grill rack, since it is important to have air flowing around the pan. Insert a meat thermometer as above and place the pan in the grill and close the cover. Cook until the fish has an internal temperature of 135° to 140°F—about 45 minutes, depending on your barbecue.

If you are serving the fish cold, allow it to cool in the cheesecloth before slicing. If you are serving it hot, cut away the cheesecloth and slice the fish into 8 to 10 servings.

# Salmon Stuffed with Couscous and Smoked Salmon

Makes 4 to 8 servings, depending on the size of the fish

**Max:** *This preparation shows off salmon in two ways—fresh and smoked.*

**Lora:** *You can cook the couscous either in water or in fish broth (available in the freezer case of many gourmet stores and markets). If you've never made it before, this is a good introduction. You can use it instead of rice or the other usual starches for any meal.*

## For the stuffing

2 tablespoons butter

1 large shallot, chopped

1 cup water or fish stock

½ cup uncooked couscous

1 cup packed fresh Italian parsley leaves, chopped

Juice and finely chopped zest of 1 large lemon

4 ounces smoked salmon, cut into 1-inch pieces

Freshly ground black pepper to taste

## To complete

Eight 5- to 6-ounce or four coho salmon, boned, butterflied, heads on, rinsed and patted dry, 8 ounces

2 tablespoons butter, melted

Butcher's string, soaked in water for several minutes (for easy removal after cooking)

2 to 3 tablespoons fresh lemon juice

⅓ cup dry white wine

To make the stuffing, in a small saucepan over moderate heat, melt the butter. Add the shallot and cook, stirring, until softened. Add the water or fish stock and bring to a rapid boil. Add the couscous, cover, and remove the pan from the heat. Allow the couscous to rest, covered, for 5 minutes, then lift the lid and fluff the grains with a fork. Mix in the parsley and lemon juice and zest, then let cool completely before mixing in the smoked salmon. Season with pepper. The smoked salmon will make it salty enough.

Lay the salmon, open, skin side down, on the work surface. Divide the stuffing evenly between the fish, adding about ½ cup to the small fish or ⅔ cup to the large fish. Fold the fillets closed over the stuffing, push down to "seal" the opening (some stuffing may squeeze out—that's fine; either stuff it back in or discard it). Brush the fish generously with the melted butter. Cut the butcher's string into 8-inch lengths and use three lengths on each fillet to tie it closed. Place the fish in a large ovenproof baking dish and add the lemon juice and wine. The fish can be refrigerated at this point for up to 4 hours.

Preheat the oven to 400°F with the rack set in the upper third but not at the highest position in the oven.

Bake the fish, uncovered, until a knife inserted in the center comes out hot and the fillets flake easily, about 30 minutes.

To serve, cut the strings and slide them out. If you are using smaller fish, serve one to each person. The larger fillets should be cut in half crosswise and placed on plates. Pour any pan juices over the fillets and serve immediately.

# Commander's Palace Tasso-Stuffed Shrimp

Makes 6 to 8 servings

*We both agree that everything super-talented Chef Jamie Shannon makes is mouthwateringly delicious. This is an adaptation of an often requested recipe that's served at everyone's favorite restaurant: New Orleans' Commander's Palace.*

*Tasso is a special Cajun smoked sausage containing lean cured pork and a medley of herbs and spices. Outside of New Orleans you can find it in gourmet specialty shops and the freezer case of markets with a really good meat department. If you can't find pickled okra, you can use pickled peppers instead. The five-pepper jelly and sauce need to be prepared ahead of time. Leftover five-pepper jelly spooned over an 8-ounce block of cream cheese makes a great (and easy) cocktail spread. Use any leftover spicy mayonnaise in potato salad or instead of regular mayonnaise when making a sandwich.*

## For the five-pepper jelly

⅓ cup honey

⅔ cup white vinegar

1 each red, green, and yellow bell peppers, seeded and diced

1 jalapeño pepper, seeded and sliced (wear rubber gloves for this)

¼ teaspoon freshly ground black pepper

Salt to taste

## For the spicy mayonnaise

1½ cups mayonnaise

⅓ cup relish

10 drops Tabasco sauce

Place the honey and vinegar in a medium-size nonreactive saucepan over moderate heat, bring to a simmer, and cook down until the mixture is thick and sticky. Add the remaining jelly ingredients and cook until the peppers are soft. Season with salt. Set aside.

Mix together the spicy-mayonnaise ingredients in a medium-size mixing bowl.

Make a ¼-inch-deep incision down the back of each shrimp and place one strip of tasso in each incision. Secure with a toothpick. Mix the flour together with the dried herbs and dredge the shrimp in the mixture, tapping off any excess. Heat 3 inches of vegetable oil in a large skillet and fry the shrimp until crisp and golden. Drain on paper towels.

## For the shrimp

36 jumbo shrimp, shelled and deveined

6 ounces spicy tasso, cut into 1-inch julienne strips

½ cup all-purpose flour

1 teaspoon dried basil

1 teaspoon dried marjoram

1 teaspoon dried oregano

Vegetable oil for frying

36 pickled okra or 1½-by-1-inch strips pickled peppers

To assemble, spread the five-pepper jelly on the bottom of each serving plate. Arrange the fried shrimp on the plate, alternating with the okra or pickled peppers. Garnish with the spicy mayonnaise.

# Shrimp in Tomato Baskets

Makes **8** servings

*Fresh lemon and toasted sesame oil perfume this cold seafood salad. Try to use perfectly ripe, flavorful tomatoes.*

2 pounds small or medium-size shrimp, cooked

1 large cucumber, peeled, halved lengthwise, seeded, and thinly sliced

2 cups shredded green cabbage

1 small red onion, finely diced

2 tablespoons sesame seeds, toasted (see Note)

¼ cup minced fresh coriander (cilantro) leaves

½ cup rice vinegar (available in gourmet food stores and many large supermarkets)

⅓ cup honey

2 tablespoons soy sauce

2 tablespoons peeled and grated fresh ginger root

2 tablespoons mild toasted sesame oil (available in gourmet food stores and many large supermarkets)

1 cup chow-mein noodles

4 large ripe tomatoes

If you are using medium-size shrimp, cut them into thirds. In a large mixing bowl, combine the shrimp, cucumber, cabbage, onion, sesame seeds, and fresh coriander and toss well. In a medium-size mixing bowl, whisk together the vinegar, honey, soy sauce, ginger root, and sesame oil. Pour this mixture over the shrimp mixture and toss well. Gently stir in the noodles

Cut each tomato in half crosswise. With a grapefruit spoon, scoop out the seeds and pulp to form a shell. Fill with a generous portion of the shrimp salad and serve on a lettuce-lined platter.

**Note:** To toast sesame seeds, add the seeds to a large, heavy-bottomed skillet. Place the skillet over medium-high heat and cook, stirring or shaking the pan constantly until the seeds are deep golden brown. Immediately empty the seeds onto a paper towel–lined sheet pan to cool.

# Poultry and Meat

# Prosciutto and Jack Cheese–Stuffed Chicken Breasts

Makes 4 servings

**Max:** *I like the combination of flavors and textures in this recipe. The presentation is attractive—spirals of chicken wrapped around the stuffing.*

**Lora:** *I like the fact that it can be served hot as well as cold.*

4 whole boneless, skinless chicken breasts, cut in half

4 thin slices prosciutto

4 thin slices Monterey Jack cheese, plain or with jalapeños

1 large red onion, thinly sliced

Olive oil

½ teaspoon salt

½ teaspoon freshly ground black pepper

Preheat the oven to 350°F with the rack set in the center position.

Place each half chicken breast between two 8-inch squares of plastic wrap. With the bottom of a small sauté pan, pound the chicken until it is about ⅛ inch thick. Remove the top layer of the plastic wrap and place one slice each of the prosciutto and cheese on top of the chicken, then place a slice of onion on top of the cheese. Roll the chicken lengthwise to form a cylinder. Cut 4 lengths of kitchen string. Tie the chicken roll-up 3 times crosswise, once lengthwise, to secure the roll. Repeat with the other chicken-breast halves and place in a baking dish. Lightly oil the chicken and season with the salt and pepper. Cook the chicken, uncovered, for 35 minutes, then allow it to rest for 10 minutes before cutting and removing the string. Use a sharp knife to cut each piece on the diagonal into 4 or 5 pieces. Serve hot or cold.

# Roast Turkey Stuffed with Cornbread, Pecans, and Cranberries Two Ways

**Serves:**
The cavity-stuffed turkey will serve ten to twelve, the boned rolled breast about eight people.

*Max: Here's a traditional Thanksgiving recipe with a choice of preparations; you can stuff the cavity of the turkey, or stuff and roll a boneless turkey breast. The same amount of stuffing is used in both preparations.*

*Lora: Yummm! This is the best. In our house we always make twice as much stuffing as we need, just to ensure that there are leftovers.*

*Max: Hey, Mom, remember the time you forgot to take the giblets and other stuff in the little bag out of the turkey?*

*Lora: Shut up, Max.*

### For the stuffing

4 to 6 corn muffins, or enough to make 6 cups crumbs, or 6 cups unseasoned dry corn-bread stuffing

1½ cups (1½ sticks) butter

1 large Spanish onion, diced

2 large stalks celery, diced

2 cups pecan halves, coarsely chopped

1 cup dried cranberries

Finely grated rind of 1 large orange

Salt and freshly ground black pepper to taste

### For the whole turkey

One 10-to-12-pound fresh or defrosted frozen turkey

2 large onions, thickly sliced

To make the stuffing, preheat the oven to 375°F with the rack set in the upper position. Crumble the muffins, and scatter the crumbs in a single layer in a large shallow roasting pan. Bake until lightly toasted, 10 to 12 minutes. Cool slightly. Melt the butter in a large skillet, then cook the onion and celery, stirring, until translucent. Pour the butter and vegetables over the crumbs, add the remaining stuffing ingredients, and stir just to combine.

To make a whole turkey, preheat the oven to 350°F with the rack set in the center position. Spray a large heavy roasting pan with nonfat vegetable spray. Remove the giblets from the neck of the turkey, rinse the turkey inside and outside, and pat dry with paper towels. Set the turkey in the pan breast side up. Use a large spoon to fill the cavity loosely with the stuffing. The remaining stuffing can be

2 carrots, thickly sliced

½ cup (1 stick) butter, very soft

4 to 6 cups chicken broth

Salt and pepper to taste

### For the turkey roll

½ cup (1 stick) butter, softened

2 cups orange juice

One 5½-to-6-pound turkey breast, boned and butterflied (ask your butcher to do this)

3 cups chicken broth

2 large onions, thickly sliced

2 carrots, thickly sliced

Salt and pepper to taste

divided between the neck area and a buttered ovenproof casserole. Tie the turkey's legs together with kitchen string. If you wish, you can use a trussing kit (available in the supermarket) to close the cavity securely. Add the onions and carrots to the pan. Rub the turkey with the butter and add 3 cups of the broth to the pan, reserving the rest for basting. Roast the turkey 25 minutes per pound, basting frequently with the remaining broth, until an instant-read meat thermometer registers 180°F when inserted in the thickest parts of the thigh and breast. The leftover stuffing in the casserole can be covered and cooked during the last hour of the turkey's roasting. Remove the cover during the last 15 minutes of cooking and baste with the turkey's pan juices.

Remove the turkey from the oven and immediately remove the stuffing to a warm serving dish. Allow the turkey to rest for 15 minutes, then slice the meat onto a platter. Discard the carrots and onions. Pour off the pan juices into a clear glass measuring cup, skim off the fat, and season with salt and pepper before serving along with the turkey.

To make the turkey roll, preheat the oven to 350°F with the rack set in the center position. Spray a large heavy roasting pan with nonfat vegetable spray. Lay the turkey breast on a large piece of dampened cheesecloth on your work surface and cover it with a large piece of plastic wrap. Use a heavy skillet to pound the turkey lightly to as uniform a thickness as possible. Remove the plastic wrap. Scatter half to two thirds of the stuffing over the surface of the turkey (the remainder will be cooked in a buttered overproof casserole). Using the cheesecloth to help you, roll the turkey from one of the longer sides (you might need someone to help you with this step). Secure the roll at 2-inch intervals with kitchen string and tie together the ends of the cheesecloth. Place the roll in the prepared pan and coat it on all sides generously with the butter. Add the orange juice, 2 cups of the broth, and the onions and carrots to the pan. Place the remaining stuffing in an ovenproof casserole.

**77  Poultry and Meat**

*continued*

Roast the turkey 20 minutes per pound, basting frequently with the remaining broth, until an instant-read meat thermometer inserted in the center registers 180°F. During the final hour of the cooking, place the covered casserole in the oven, removing the cover and basting with the turkey's juices during the last 15 to 20 minutes of cooking. Remove the roll from the oven and allow it to rest for 10 minutes before removing the string and cheesecloth and cutting it into 1½-inch-thick slices. Skim the fat off the pan juices, season with salt and pepper, and pass separately.

# Jumbo Corn Muffins Stuffed with Jerk Chicken

Makes **6** servings

**Lora:** *Spicy, tender pieces of chile-stewed chicken are cradled in individual corn-muffin cups. You'll need a jumbo-muffin tin to make these.*

**Max:** *If you don't like your foods quite as hot and spicy as called for here, you can turn the heat down on this recipe by halving the amounts of chili powder and chipotle peppers.*

## For the muffins

¾ cup all-purpose flour

¾ cup yellow cornmeal

2 teaspoons baking powder

½ teaspoon baking soda

½ teaspoon salt

1½ teaspoons chili powder

¾ cup sour cream

2 large eggs

¼ cup (½ stick) butter, melted

½ cup finely grated jack or Cheddar cheese

## For the jerk chicken

1½ pounds chicken tenders, tendons removed

1 medium-size onion, cut into 8 pieces

1 teaspoon chopped canned chipotle chiles, or more to taste

½ teaspoon ground allspice

2 teaspoons prepared mustard

1 teaspoon freshly ground black pepper

1 tablespoon balsamic vinegar

1 tablespoon soy sauce

1 tablespoon vegetable oil

Preheat the oven to 400°F with the rack set in the center position. Generously butter a 6-hole jumbo-muffin tin. In a medium-size mixing bowl, stir together the flour, cornmeal, baking powder, baking soda, salt, and chili powder. Place the sour cream, eggs, and melted butter in small mixing bowl and stir to blend until smooth. Stir in the cheese, then add the wet ingredients to the dry, stirring just to mix. (Overmixing will make for tough muffins.) Divide the batter among the 6 cups. Bake until a cake tester or toothpick inserted in the center comes out clean, 20 to 24 minutes. Cool in the pan for 5 minutes, then remove to a wire rack to cool completely.

Reduce the heat in the oven to 375°F with the rack set in the upper third but not at the highest position. Place the chicken in an ovenproof baking dish. Stir together the remaining jerk-chicken ingredients and pour them over the chicken. Cover the dish with a sheet of aluminum foil and bake for 45 minutes.

To assemble, use a serrated knife to slice off the top quarter of the muffins. Use a teaspoon to scoop out a small well in the center. Place the muffins in a small bowl or rimmed plate and spoon the jerk chicken over the muffins (it will overflow the sides and pool around the bottom of the muffins), replace the top, and serve hot.

# Roasted Turkey with Jambalaya Stuffing

**Makes 8 servings**

**Lora:** *Thanks for this recipe goes to Paul McIlhenny, whose Tabasco sauce lights up the world.*

**Max:** *When I was cooking in New Orleans, Mr. McIlhenny invited me and my mother down to his fishing camp near Avery Island for a crawfish boil. To this day I still dream of crawfish piled two feet high on a picnic table and the bunch of us eating like there was no tomorrow.*

One 12-pound fresh or frozen turkey, completely thawed

### For the stuffing

One 12-ounce package bulk pork sausage

3 celery stalks, diced

1 large red bell pepper, seeded and diced

4 large scallions, green and white parts, sliced

½ pound cooked ham, diced

½ cup chopped fresh parsley leaves

2 teaspoons Tabasco sauce

1 teaspoon salt

1 teaspoon dried thyme

6 cups cooked long-grain rice

1 cup chicken broth or water

2 large eggs, lightly beaten

### For roasting

Vegetable oil or melted butter or margarine

One 15½-ounce can chicken broth

1 large onion, thickly sliced

Remove the giblets and neck from the turkey and rinse it well under cold running water. Pat dry with paper towels.

To make the stuffing, in a large skillet over moderately high heat, cook the pork sausage until well browned, stirring frequently to break up the meat. Using a slotted spoon, remove the sausage to large bowl. In the drippings remaining in the skillet, cook the celery and red pepper over moderate heat until softened, stirring occasionally. Add the scallions, ham, parsley, Tabasco sauce, salt, and thyme. Cook 1 minute longer, then add to the sausage mixture in the bowl along with the cooked rice, chicken broth, and eggs.

Preheat the oven to 325°F. Fill the neck cavity of the turkey lightly with stuffing. Fold the neck skin over the stuffing and fasten with 1 or 2 skewers. Place the turkey breast side up on a rack set in a large heavy roasting pan. Fill the body cavity with stuffing, packing it loosely. Put any extra stuffing in a buttered baking dish and bake it with the turkey during the last hour or cooking. With kitchen string, tie the legs together. Brush the turkey lightly with the vegetable oil or melted butter or margarine, add the can of

**For Spicy Pan Gravy**
1½ cups water
¾ cup chicken broth or water
½ teaspoon Tabasco sauce
Salt to taste

chicken broth and the onion to the bottom of the pan, and cover loosely with a sheet of aluminum foil. Roast the bird until an instant-read meat thermometer inserted deep into the thigh, but not touching the bone, reads 180°F, about 4 hours, basting every 20 minutes with drippings from the pan. Remove the turkey to a serving platter, remove the stuffing immediately, and then let the turkey stand for 20 minutes so the juices can settle before carving.

While the bird is resting, prepare the gravy: Remove the rack from the roasting pan. Skim the fat from the drippings in the pan. Add the water to the pan and stir to loosen the brown bits off the bottom. Pour into a small saucepan; add the chicken broth and Tabasco sauce, and season with salt. Heat to boiling over high heat, stirring constantly. Serve separately.

# Roast Capon with Oyster-Cracker Stuffing

**Max:** *Mom got all excited, thinking she'd created a break-through in stuffing, until I pointed out that folks have been using oyster crackers as a basis for stuffing since the Stone Ages.*

**Lora:** *Be that as it may, having tasted chicken stuffed this way, I'll never go back to Ritz crackers.*

**Max:** *Speaking of weaning yourself from Ritz crackers, this is also a great stuffing to use in lobster.*

One 5-to-6-pound capon or very large roasting chicken

½ cup (1 stick) butter

1 cup diced onions

1 cup diced celery

1 tablespoon fresh rosemary leaves, or 1 teaspoon dried

⅔ cup chicken broth

3 cups oyster crackers

½ teaspoon freshly ground black pepper

Preheat the oven to 375°F with the rack set in the center position. Butter a baking dish or spray it with nonstick vegetable spray. Remove the giblets from inside the capon, reserving the neck. Rinse the cavity and dry it with paper towels. Melt the butter in a medium-size skillet over moderate heat and cook the diced onions and celery together, stirring, until golden brown. In a large mixing bowl, combine the cooked onions and celery and their cooking juices, the rosemary, broth, oyster crackers, and pepper. Stir to coat the crackers completely with the liquid. Let the stuffing rest 5 to 7 minutes to allow the crackers to absorb some of the liquid.

Place three quarters of the stuffing in the capon's cavity, mounding it slightly at the opening. Tie the legs together with kitchen string to keep the stuffing in place. Place the remaining stuffing in the neck cavity, then pull the flap of skin down over it. Insert a meat thermometer deep into the thigh (but not so deep it touches a bone), and roast the capon until the thermometer reads 185°F, 2 to 2½ hours.

Immediately spoon the stuffing into a warmed serving dish, carve the capon, and serve hot.

# Fig-Stuffed Cornish Game Hens

**Makes 6 servings**

**Lora:** *The summer Max was eight, we rented a house in a tiny hill town in the south of France. He was the only one in the family with any command of French (the result of years in Montessori school, where I thought he was only learning to wash tables). Max was commandeered into going to the marché to act as translator. This was one of the dishes we made in our farmhouse kitchen that spring in Provence.*

**Max:** *I'll bet there aren't many eight-year-old American kids who know the French for "I'm not related to this lady standing next to me."*

6 cornish game hens

Salt and freshly ground black pepper

6 thin slices prosciutto

6 figs, preferably fresh, stems cut

½ cup (1 stick) butter, melted

½ cup dry white wine

2 tablespoons chopped fresh parsley leaves

Preheat the oven to 325°F with the rack set in the center position. Butter an ovenproof casserole or spray it with nonstick vegetable spray. Season the hens inside and out with salt and pepper. Wrap a slice of prosciutto around each fig and tuck it into the hen's cavity. Place the birds in a large baking dish, breast side up. Drizzle with the butter, then add the wine. Cover and bake for 1½ hours. Remove the cover, turn the oven temperature up to 500°F, and cook until well browned, about another 10 minutes. Drizzle with the pan juices, sprinkle with the parsley, and serve hot.

# Duck Breast Stuffed with Ginger, Coriander, and Lemon

**Max:** *Boneless, skinless duck breasts lend themselves perfectly to stuffing. After the small rolls are marinated, they can be oven-roasted or cooked on the grill. This recipe and the one that follows are two examples of how delicious such a preparation can be. After you get the hang of it, try making up your own stuffings.*

**Lora:** *Boned duck breasts can be special-ordered from the meat section of many supermarkets, and are often available fresh in meat markets.*

**Makes 4 servings**

## For the marinade

One 1-ounce piece fresh ginger (about 2½ by 1 inch), peeled and cut into very thin strips

3 tablespoons soy sauce

3 tablespoons balsamic vinegar

2 tablespoons firmly packed dark-brown sugar

¼ cup water

One 3-inch piece lemongrass (available in Asian markets and many whole-food stores), outer leaves peeled, stem end cut, and sliced in half vertically

¼ cup loosely packed fresh coriander (cilantro) leaves

2 tablespoons mild toasted sesame oil (available in gourmet food stores and many large supermarkets)

Place all the marinade ingredients in a small saucepan set over moderate heat. Bring to a rapid simmer and cook until the ginger is very soft, about 15 minutes. Cool completely. Remove the ginger and reserve both it and the liquid.

Place the duck breast on a work surface and locate the side that is thicker (it will be the side that was attached to the other breast). With a very sharp knife (a paring knife works well), carefully slice the breast horizontally about three quarters of the way through, so it can be opened like a book and laid flat. Don't worry if you make a hole or two in the meat.

Combine the lemon zest, brown sugar, vinegar, and reserved ginger in a small mixing bowl. Mash them together with a spoon until they are well combined and form a thin paste. Soak twelve 6-inch lengths of butcher's string in water. Spread about a tablespoon of the paste over the center of the cut side of each duck breast. Top with a quarter of the ginger. (Remember, the ginger is spicy, so use less if you want to cut some of the heat.) Starting with one

## To prepare the duck

2 whole duck breasts (about 1 pound total), boned, skinned, and cut into 4 halves

## To complete

Finely grated zest of 1 large lemon

2 tablespoons firmly packed dark-brown sugar

1 tablespoon balsamic vinegar

3 tablespoons vegetable oil

long side, roll the breast up jelly-roll style and tie it securely with 3 pieces of string spaced to keep the roll together. Add any leftover filling to the marinade and place the duck breasts in the marinade. Cover and marinate, refrigerated, for at least 2 hours and as long as 12 hours.

To roast, preheat the oven to 425°F with the rack set in the upper third but not at the highest position. Select a shallow heavy-duty ovenproof baking dish and add 2 tablespoons of the vegetable oil to it. Place the dish in the oven while it preheats. Remove the duck from the marinade and dry it very well with paper towels. Place the duck breasts in the hot dish, at least 2 inches apart, and place in the oven. After 10 minutes, turn the duck so the seared side is up. Cook until the duck has an internal temperature of 120°F as registered on an instant-read meat thermometer, another 7 to 10 minutes. If you don't want rare duck, cook to a temperature of 140°F.

To grill, cook the duck on a preheated grill for 15 minutes, turning once or twice to make sure the outside is completely browned and the internal temperature is 120°F for rare and 140°F for well done.

Heat the marinade in a small saucepan until it simmers and cook for 5 minutes. Allow the duck to rest for 5 minutes before removing the string and slicing each breast half on the diagonal into 5 or 6 pieces. To serve, lay the pieces slightly overlapping one another on each dinner plate and add a tablespoon of the marinade.

# Duck Breast Stuffed with Sour Cherries

Makes 4 servings

**Lora:** *Dried sour cherries and mango chutney are easy to find in gourmet stores as well as many supermarkets. They give this duck preparation an elegant zing that is tempered by a sweet-and-sour marinade.*

**Max:** *Use a very sharp, thin knife to slice the duck breasts so that the meat keeps its shape and the filling doesn't fall out. This dish calls for a big red wine like a Barolo or a nice Chianti.*

### For the stuffing

½ cup dried sour cherries (2 ounces)

⅓ cup Grand Marnier or other orange liqueur, or orange juice

2 whole duck breasts (about 1 pound total), boned, skinned, and cut into 4 halves

### For the marinade

3 tablespoons mango chutney

½ cup orange juice

½ teaspoon ground ginger

2 tablespoons soy sauce

### To roast

2 tablespoons vegetable oil

Place the cherries and liquid in a small nonreactive saucepan over moderate heat and stir to blend. When the liquid starts to simmer, reduce the heat to low and cook for 3 minutes, stirring once or twice. Remove the pan from the heat, cover, and allow the cherries to cool at room temperature for 15 to 20 minutes.

Place the duck breasts on your work surface and locate the side that is thicker (it will be the side that was attached to the other breast). With a very sharp knife (a paring knife works well), carefully slice the breast horizontally about three quarters of the way through, so it can be opened like a book and laid flat. Don't worry if you make a hole or two in the meat. Cover with plastic wrap and refrigerate while you prepare the marinade.

Place the marinade ingredients in a heavy-duty zippered-top plastic bag bowl and shake to combine. Take the duck out of the refrigerator. Soak twelve 6-inch lengths of butcher's string in water. Place about 1½ tablespoons of the cherries down the length of the center of each breast. Starting with one long side, roll the breast jelly-roll style and tie it securely with three pieces of string spaced to keep the roll together. Add any leftover filling to the marinade and place the duck breasts in the plastic bag. Marinate, refrigerated, for at least 2 hours and as long as 12 hours.

To roast, preheat the oven to 425°F with the rack set in the upper third but not at the highest position. Select a shallow heavy-duty ovenproof baking dish, add the vegetable oil to it, and place the pan in the oven while it preheats. Remove the duck from the marinade and dry it very well with paper towels. Place the duck breasts in the hot dish at least 2 inches apart and place in the oven. After 10 minutes, turn the duck so the seared side is up. Cook until the duck has an internal temperature of 120°F as measured on an instant-read meat thermometer, another 7 to 10 minutes. If you don't want rare duck, cook to a temperature of 140°F.

To grill, cook the duck on a preheated grill for 15 minutes, turning once or twice to make sure the outside is completely browned and the internal temperature is 120°F for rare and 140°F for well done.

Heat the marinade in a small saucepan until it simmers and cook for 5 minutes. Allow the duck to rest for 5 minutes before removing the string and slicing each breast half on the diagonal into 5 or 6 pieces. To serve, lay the pieces slightly overlapping on each dinner plate and add a tablespoon of the marinade.

# Lamb Spirals Stuffed with Roasted Garlic and Goat Cheese

Makes **4** servings

**Max:** *This dish was inspired by some time I spent in Greece a few summers ago. The Greeks made this with goat, but I think it's more realistic to use lamb in the United States. It's important to use an instant-read meat thermometer to tell when the meat is cooked to your satisfaction, because everything depends on the heat of your broiler and the distance between the meat and the broiler element.*

**Lora:** *Ask your butcher to prepare the lamb loins; then you get to do the fun part.*

1 large head garlic

⅔ cup olive oil

½ cup pine nuts, toasted (see Note, page 49)

8 ounces goat cheese (plain or herbed)

2 lamb loins (¾ to 1 pound each), boned, butterflied, and pounded thin

Pinch of salt

Pinch of freshly ground black pepper

1 tablespoon chopped fresh Italian parsley leaves

Preheat the oven to 300°F with the rack set in the upper third. Place the garlic head in a small ovenproof ramekin and add the olive oil to coat. Cover with a sheet of aluminum foil and bake until the garlic is deep golden brown, about 1 hour. Cool, then squeeze each garlic clove out of its peel into a mixing bowl. Mix in ¼ cup of the oil in which the garlic cooked. Stir in the pine nuts, then the goat cheese, mixing until well combined.

Place the lamb pieces flat on your work surface. Season with the salt and pepper. Spread the garlic stuffing evenly over the surface, roll up the lamb and tie at intervals with kitchen butcher's string. Place the pieces on a baking sheet.

Preheat the broiler to high with the rack set in the upper third of the oven. Broil until the tops of the loins are well browned, about 5 minutes, then give them a one-third turn and cook another 4 or 5 minutes. Repeat once more and test the internal temperature with an instant-read meat thermometer; it should be 110°F for very rare, and 120°F for medium rare. Allow the lamb to rest for 10 minutes before removing the string and slicing. Garnish with the chopped parsley. Serve hot or at room temperature.

# Garlic and Olive–Stuffed Butterflied Leg of Lamb

**Makes 4 servings**

*Garlic, rosemary, and Kalamata olives perfume this lamb preparation from the Provence area of southern France. Ask in advance and your butcher will butterfly the lamb for you.*

One 2-pound boneless leg of lamb, butterflied

¼ cup garlic cloves, peeled, left whole if small, cut in half lengthwise if large

⅓ cup pitted Kalamata olives, cut in half lengthwise

2 tablespoons fresh rosemary leaves

3 tablespoons olive oil

2 tablespoon soy sauce

2 tablespoons balsamic vinegar

Lay the lamb open on your work surface. Use a small, sharp knife to cut 1-inch-deep pockets at a shallow angle into the surface of both sides of the meat. Slip either a piece of garlic or an olive into each slit, alternating as often as possible. Use your finger to push the garlic or olive deep into the slit, then close the meat around it. Don't worry about using up every last piece of garlic and olive.

In a small mixing bowl, combine the rosemary, olive oil, soy sauce, vinegar, and any remaining garlic and olives. Place the lamb in a shallow baking dish. Pour the mixture over to coat both sides. Cover the dish with plastic wrap and refrigerate for at least 6 hours and as long as 24 hours. The meat can also be marinated in a large zippered-top plastic bag.

Preheat the broiler to high with the rack set in the upper third but not at the highest position in the oven. Drain the meat, place it in a broiler-safe dish, and position 5 to 6 inches away from the element. Broil for 12 to 15 minutes (the longer, the more well done), then turn and broil for another 12 to 15 minutes. Use an instant-read meat thermometer to test for doneness: 110°F for very rare, 120°F for medium rare, and 130°F for medium. You can also barbecue the lamb on a preheated grill, using the same cooking times.

To serve, cut the meat into thin slices and serve hot, warm, or cold.

# Stuffed Cabbage Rolls with Yogurt Dill Sauce

Makes 4 servings

**Lora:** *Instead of boiling cabbage to soften the leaves, try placing the head in the freezer for a couple of hours. When you pull it out and it defrosts, the leaves are pliable enough to wrap, and your kitchen doesn't smell like cooking cabbage.*

**Max:** *I'm sure glad you figured out the tip for wilting the cabbage leaves without boiling them. I remember that I wouldn't eat stuffed cabbage when I was little because of the way the kitchen smelled when Grandma was boiling the leaves.*

1 large head green cabbage (about 3 pounds), cored

2 tablespoons olive oil

3 large scallions, sliced

2 large cloves garlic, minced

1 pound ground lamb

2 cups plain yogurt, divided

¼ cup chopped fresh dill, divided

1½ teaspoons Tabasco sauce

1½ teaspoons salt

1 cup chicken or beef broth

One 10-ounce can stewed tomatoes

Prepare the cabbage as described in the headnote above. Or, if you prefer to cook it, bring a large pot of water to a rapid boil. Add the cabbage cored end down. Reduce the heat to moderate, cover, and simmer until leaves are softened, 10 to 12 minutes. Remove the cabbage to a bowl of cold water to stop the cooking.

Separate 16 large leaves from the head of cabbage. Trim the tough ribs on the back of the leaves so that they will roll up easily. Chop enough of the remaining cabbage to make 3 cups.

Heat the oil in a large skillet, then cook the chopped cabbage, scallions, and garlic together until softened, about 10 minutes, stirring occasionally. Use a slotted spoon to remove the cabbage to a large mixing bowl. Increase the heat under the skillet to high, add the lamb, and cook until it is well browned and no pink remains, stirring frequently. Combine the lamb with the cabbage mixture. Mix together the lamb, ½ cup of the yogurt, 2 tablespoons of the dill, the Tabasco sauce, and salt.

Preheat the oven to 400°F. Place 3 tablespoons of the lamb mixture at bottom of a cabbage leaf and roll it up tightly to form a 3-inch-long roll, tucking the ends in as you roll. Repeat with the remaining lamb mixture and leaves. Place the rolled leaves on a rack set in a large roasting pan. Add the broth and the tomatoes with their liquid. Cover the pan tightly with a sheet of aluminum foil and bake until the rolls are hot, about 30 minutes.

Meanwhile, in a medium-size bowl, combine the remaining 1½ cups yogurt and 2 tablespoons dill. When the rolls are done, remove them to a platter. Pour the pan juices into a small saucepan over high heat, reduce the liquid by a third, then pour over the rolls. Pass the yogurt sauce separately.

# Tex-Mex Stuffed Meat Loaf

**Makes 6 generous servings**

*We had people gathered around the oven waiting for this to be finished. The smell was intoxicating. We kept explaining that it was "just meat loaf," but no one seemed to care. I've never seen a humble dish like this disappear so fast. Nacho-cheese sauce can be found right next to the bottled salsa on the supermarket shelf.*

1½ pounds lean ground beef

1 small onion, diced

2 large eggs

½ cup dried plain bread crumbs

¼ cup Worcestershire sauce

3 tablespoons Dijon mustard

1 teaspoon salt

½ teaspoon freshly ground black pepper

2 tablespoons canned chopped green chiles (optional)

1 cup drained canned roasted red peppers and cut in 1-inch pieces

½ cup nacho-cheese sauce

½ cup bottled salsa

Preheat the oven to 375°F with the rack set in the center position. With an electric mixer or by hand in a large mixing bowl, combine ground beef with the onion, eggs, bread crumbs, Worcestershire sauce, mustard, salt, and pepper. Grease a 9-by-5-by-3-inch loaf pan with nonstick vegetable spray and pack half the meat mixture in the bottom. Make a 1-inch-deep well in the mixture running the length of the loaf pan, leaving ½ inch on all sides. In the well make a layer of the green chiles, top that with a layer of the red peppers, and top that with the cheese. Pack the rest of the meat mixture on top, pushing the sides down with your fingers to create a mound. Evenly spread the salsa on top of the loaf and bake until an instant-read meat thermometer registers 130°F when inserted in the center, or a knife inserted in the center comes out hot, about 1 hour. After baking, pour off any accumulated liquid from the top of the loaf. Slice and serve hot or cool. It makes the world's best meat-loaf sandwiches.

# Beef Fajitas

Makes 4 servings

**Max:** *This one is a big hit in my brother's Mexican restaurant in Taiwan. You can substitute beef or chicken broth for sherry if you prefer not to cook with wine, as well as chicken tenders for the beef.*

**Lora:** *That's right, folks. A Mexican restaurant in Taiwan.*

2 tablespoons vegetable oil

⅓ cup dry sherry

1 large onion, sliced

1 cup sliced mushrooms

1½ pounds sirloin tip, fat trimmed, cut into 2-by-1-inch strips

2 serrano or jalapeño chiles, seeded and minced (wear gloves to do this)

½ teaspoon ground cumin

¼ teaspoon ground coriander

1 teaspoon dried cilantro, or 1 tablespoon fresh coriander (cilantro) leaves

4 large flour tortillas

½ cup bottled salsa

½ ripe avocado, peeled, pitted, and thinly sliced

1 cup sour cream

Heat the oil and sherry together in a large skillet over moderate heat, then cook the onion and mushrooms together, stirring, until quite soft, about 10 minutes. Add the steak to the skillet, and cook until the meat is almost cooked through, 3 to 4 minutes. Add the chiles, cumin, coriander, and cilantro, and cook another 3 minutes, stirring frequently.

Warm the tortillas in the toaster oven or conventional oven, or in the microwave in a plastic bag. Place the mushrooms and meat in a serving dish. Arrange the salsa, sliced avocado, and sour cream in bowls. Place the tortillas in a napkin-lined basket, and have your guests fill their own.

# Butterflied Flank Steak Stuffed with Grainy Mustard, Prosciutto, and Tarragon

Makes **4** servings

*This filled, rolled, marinated, and oven-roasted flank steak makes a stunning presentation with its spirals of meat and filling. The combination of flavors and textures is remarkable. If there are any leftovers (doubtful), this is also great served cold.*

One 1¼-to-1½-pound flank steak

2 tablespoons grainy mustard such as Pommery

1 tablespoon chopped fresh tarragon leaves

4 very thin slices prosciutto or Black Forest ham

## For the marinade

4 garlic cloves, crushed

½ cup olive oil

¼ cup Worcestershire sauce

2 tablespoons grainy mustard such as Pommery

1 teaspoon salt

You can ask your butcher to butterfly the steak, but you can easily do it yourself if you have a very sharp knife. Lay the steak on your work surface. One long side will be slightly thicker than the other. Slice down the full length of this side horizontally, as you would cut a cake into 2 layers. Cut almost to the other side, leaving about 1 inch still connected. Don't worry if you make a hole, or cut through the "seam" in a place or two. Open the steak like a book, with the seam in the center. Spread the steak evenly with the mustard, sprinkle with the tarragon leaves, and then cover with the ham slices, overlapping their edges if necessary.

Soak four 10-inch lengths of butcher's string briefly in water (this keeps them from sticking when you remove them after cooking). Starting with a long edge, roll up the steak jelly-roll style. Tie it at 2-to-3-inch intervals with the wet string.

Combine the marinade ingredients in a large, heavy-duty zippered-top plastic bag. Add the steak, seal the top, shake to coat, and refrigerate for at least 2 hours or as long as 12 hours.

Preheat the oven to 450°F with the rack set in the center position. Select an ovenproof pan that can also go on the stovetop. Remove the steak from the marinade and pat it dry with paper towels. Pour the marinade into a glass measuring cup. Remove about 2 tablespoons of oil from the top and add it to the pan. Place the pan over high heat and, when the oil is hot, add the steak and sear it, turning frequently, until all its sides are browned. This will take 2 to 3 minutes per side. Insert a meat thermometer into the center of the roll and place the pan in the hot oven. Roast until the thermometer registers 120°F, 14 to 18 minutes. Remove the steak and allow it to rest for 5 minutes before removing the string and slicing on a diagonal into 1-inch-thick pieces. Heat the remaining marinade, spoon a little over the slices, and serve hot.

# Pork Loin Stuffed with Fruit and Nuts

*Dried fruit is a perfect complement to roast pork. This dish is equally good hot or at room temperature and makes a great buffet item. Have your butcher butterfly the pork for you.*

**Makes 8 servings**

## For the filling

½ cup coarsely chopped pitted California dates

¼ cup coarsely chopped dried apricots

¼ cup finely chopped pecans

1 clove garlic, minced

1½ teaspoons dried thyme, crushed

1 tablespoon molasses

¼ teaspoon salt

¼ teaspoon freshly ground black pepper

## For the roast

One 2-pound boneless pork-loin roast

2 teaspoons dried thyme

## For the glaze

⅔ cup bourbon

⅔ cup chicken broth

1 tablespoon molasses

## For the sauce

¼ cup light cream

¼ teaspoon salt

Preheat the oven to 350°F with the rack set in the center position. In a medium-size bowl, combine all the filling ingredients. Set aside. Lay the loin open and pat it flat. Spread the filling evenly over meat, roll it up like a jelly roll, and tie securely at 2-to-3-inch intervals with kitchen string. Sprinkle the surface of the roast with the thyme. Place the loin in a shallow roasting pan.

In a medium-size saucepan, combine bourbon, broth, and molasses and bring to a boil. Remove from the heat and pour over the roast. Roast the pork, uncovered, until a meat thermometer registers 160°F, about 1 hour, basting occasionally with the pan juices.

Remove the roast from pan, reserving the drippings. Cover the meat with a sheet of aluminum foil to keep it warm. Add the cream and salt to the pan drippings and cook over moderately high heat, stirring constantly, until slightly thickened. Remove the string from the roast and slice the pork, placing the slices overlapping on a platter. Pass the sauce separately.

# Vegetables

# Chile-Cheddar Rice–Stuffed Tomatoes

**Makes 6 to 10 servings**

**Lora:** *You can make this dish as hot or mild as you wish by adding more or fewer chiles and Tabasco sauce. Served hot or cold, it's a tasty main course or side vegetable.*

**Max:** *Adding some cooked corn kernels provides this dish with a sweet crunch and nice color.*

6 large or 10 medium-size flavorful tomatoes

2 tablespoons vegetable oil

1 large onion, diced

4 cloves garlic, minced

3 cups cooked white or brown rice

2 tablespoons tomato paste

One 4-ounce can mild chiles, drained and chopped

4 to 6 drops Tabasco sauce, to your taste

1½ cups grated Cheddar cheese (4 ounces)

3 tablespoons chopped fresh coriander (cilantro) leaves

Salt and freshly ground black pepper to taste

¼ cup water

Use a sharp knife to slice a little piece from the bottom of each tomato so that it will sit upright without tipping over. Cut a 2-to-3-inch-wide opening in the top of each tomato, and use a grapefruit spoon to scoop out the pulp and seeds so that you have a tomato cup. Reserve the pulp.

Heat the oil in a skillet over moderately high heat, then cook the onions, stirring, until softened and translucent. Add the garlic and cook another 2 to 3 minutes without allowing the garlic to brown.

In a large mixing bowl, toss together the onion mixture, rice, tomato paste, chiles, Tabasco, cheese, coriander, and the reserved tomato pulp. Season with salt and pepper.

Use a small spoon to scoop the stuffing into the cavity of each tomato, mounding it slightly on top.

To serve hot, preheat the oven to 325°F with the rack set in the center position. Place the tomatoes right next to each other in an ovenproof baking dish (you will probably need 2 dishes). Add the water to the dish and bake just until a cake tester or small knife inserted into the stuffing comes out hot, 15 to 20 minutes. Be careful—overcooking will cause the tomatoes to split. Serve hot or warm.

# Sausage-Stuffed Artichokes

Makes **6** servings

**Lora:** *You can use any type of link sausage in this recipe, from the traditional Italian pork sausage to the nineties-style herbed chicken and turkey sausages found in many upscale markets.*

**Max:** *This recipe is the perfect place to use up leftover rice, particularly risotto.*

6 large artichokes
⅔ pound sausage, casing removed
Olive oil, as needed
1 large onion, diced
1 cup cooked rice
1 large egg
⅓ cup grated Cheddar cheese

## To assemble
1 cup dry bread crumbs
¼ cup butter, melted, or olive oil

Bring a large pot of water to a rapid boil. Remove the stems from the artichokes (these can be cooked in the same water and eaten as a treat for the cook). Use a serrated knife to cut off the top third of the artichokes, then use scissors to snip off the ends of the leaves. Place the artichokes in the boiling water, cover, and when the water returns to the boil, reduce the heat to a gentle simmer. Cook until the insides are quite tender (you can test them by inserting a sharp knife in the center), 18 to 20 minutes. Cool the artichokes upside down in a colander.

To make the stuffing, place the sausage in a medium-size skillet over moderate heat and cook through, breaking it up into small pieces. Remove the crumbled sausage to a large mixing bowl with a slotted spoon, leaving the rendered fat in the skillet. If the skillet is on the dry side, add a few tablespoons of olive oil. Add the onion and cook, stirring, until golden brown, then add to the sausage, along with the rice, egg, and cheese. Mix well.

Preheat the oven to 400°F with the rack set in an upper but not the very highest position. Spray an ovenproof baking dish with nonstick vegetable spray, or apply a thin coating of vegetable oil.

Gently spread the inner leaves of the artichokes apart and use a grapefruit spoon to scoop out the choke (the fibrous portion) right above the heart. Pack the stuffing into each center, right to the top. Mix the bread crumbs with the butter or oil and pack evenly on top of each artichoke. The artichokes can be prepared ahead up to this point and refrigerated for as much as 24 hours covered with plastic wrap. Bake until a cake tester inserted in the center comes out hot, about 20 minutes. (Artichokes that have been refrigerated before cooking should be either brought to room temperature first or cooked 5 to 10 minutes longer.) Switch the oven to broil, and broil until the tops are brown and crisp, 3 to 4 minutes. Serve hot or at room temperature.

# Lentil-Stuffed Peppers

**Makes 8 servings**

**Max:** *You can use red, green, yellow, or even purple peppers, or a combination of colors, to make this hearty lentil dish. Be sure not to overcook the lentils, though, as they will get mushy and look pretty unappetizing.*

4 large bell peppers

### For the stuffing

2½ cups vegetable or chicken broth

1 teaspoon salt

½ teaspoon freshly ground black pepper

2 cups dried red lentils, picked over and rinsed

3 tablespoons tomato paste

¾ teaspoon ground turmeric

¾ teaspoon ground cumin

¾ teaspoon lemon pepper

4 ounces feta cheese, crumbled

Cut the peppers in half through the stem end. Cut out the seeds and any white membranes. To steam the peppers in the microwave oven, place them cut side down in a microwavable dish. Add ¼ cup water, cover with plastic wrap, and cook on high until the peppers yield to light pressure, 5 to 6 minutes. To cook on the stove top, fill a large pot with water and bring to a rapid boil. Add the peppers, reduce the heat to a moderate simmer, and cook for 3 minutes.

Allow the peppers to cool cut side down while you prepare the stuffings.

Heat the broth in a saucepan set over high heat. Add the salt and pepper, and when the liquid comes to full boil, add the lentils and reduce the heat to low. Cover the pan and cook until soft but not mushy, 10 to 15 minutes. Drain off any liquid. Stir the tomato paste and seasonings into the lentils. Divide the lentils evenly between the peppers, filling each so that it mounds slightly. Top them evenly with the feta cheese. Serve warm or at room temperature.

# Fontina-Stuffed Vidalia Onions

**Makes 4 servings**

**Lora:** *These soft, sweet onions, which caramelize during baking, combined with the melted cheese, remind me of onion soup, without the soup.*

**Max:** *This would make a terrific Thanksgiving vegetable, especially since you can prepare them ahead, bake them up to just before you add the cheese, then finish cooking them just before serving.*

4 medium-size Vidalia or other sweet onions

¼ cup olive oil

12 ounces Fontina cheese, shredded

1 cup dried bread crumbs

2 tablespoons butter, cut into 4 pieces

Preheat the oven to 400°F with the rack set in the center position. Select an ovenproof casserole large enough to fit the onions in a single layer. Peel the onions and with a grapefruit spoon or pointed teaspoon scoop out a well in the center of the onion, leaving ½ inch on the bottom and sides. Brush the onions, inside and out, with the olive oil and bake them until soft but not falling apart, about 30 minutes. Remove the casserole from the oven and reposition the rack to the upper third of the oven. Fill the centers of the onions with the Fontina cheese, then top with the bread crumbs and a pat of butter. Bake until the top is browned and the cheese bubbling, an additional 10 minutes. Serve hot.

# Baked Stuffed Zucchini

Makes **4** servings

**Lora:** *Whether you grow your own, get the surplus from a neighbor's garden, or buy them at a farmstand, freshly picked zucchini make the perfect base for a stuffed dish.*

**Max:** *Instead of regular button mushrooms, try using portobellos, shiitakes, or creminis.*

**Lora:** *How about some of those dried porcinis I brought back from Italy?*

**Max:** *I'm not wasting those on zucchini.*

4 zucchini, ½ pound each
2 tablespoons butter or margarine
2 scallions, chopped
½ pound mushrooms, chopped
½ cup pine nuts, toasted (see Note, page 49)
4 large eggs
¼ cup minced fresh parsley leaves
¼ cup chopped fresh basil leaves
1 teaspoon salt
½ teaspoon freshly ground black pepper
1 cup soft bread crumbs
½ cup grated Parmesan cheese

Preheat the oven to 350°F with the rack set in the center position. Select an ovenproof baking dish that will hold 8 lengthwise zucchini halves in one layer. Grease it with butter or margarine, or spray it with nonstick vegetable spray. Scrub the zucchini and cut each in half lengthwise. Scoop out the pulp, leaving the shells ¼ inch thick, chop the pulp finely, and set aside.

Bring a large pot of water to a rolling boil, add the zucchini shells, and simmer for 3 minutes, then remove and drain well upside down. Heat the butter or margarine in a large skillet over moderate heat, then add the zucchini pulp, scallions, and mushrooms, and cook, stirring, until the mixture is hot, about 5 minutes. Add the pine nuts and remove the skillet from the heat.

In a medium-size mixing bowl, whisk the eggs with the parsley, basil, salt, and pepper.

Add the egg mixture and bread crumbs to the pulp mixture. Spoon this mixture evenly into the zucchini shells, mounding it slightly in the middle. Top with grated cheese, then place the zucchini in the prepared baking dish, add ½ inch of water, and bake, uncovered, until the top is well browned and a knife inserted into the center comes out hot, 25 to 30 minutes. Serve hot or at room temperature.

# Germaine's Butternut Squash with Curried Rice and Chickpea Stuffing

*Butternut squash lends itself perfectly to stuffing. This fragrant recipe from our dear friend Germaine Gaudet will delight vegetarians looking for a satisfying main course. Select smaller squashes to create a novel side dish as well.*

3 large butternut squash (for main course) or 6 smaller squash (for side dish), halved, seeds scooped out and discarded

3 tablespoons vegetable oil

1 medium-size onion, diced

2 cloves garlic, finely chopped

1 generous tablespoon peeled and chopped fresh ginger

One 14-ounce can diced tomatoes with their juices

1 tablespoon honey

1½ teaspoons curry powder

1 cup rice (white or brown, as you wish), cooked al dente

One 15-ounce can chickpeas, drained

¼ cup chopped fresh coriander (cilantro) leaves

1 teaspoon salt

½ teaspoon freshly ground black pepper

Preheat the oven to 400°F with the rack set in the center position. Place the squash cut sides down in a large baking dish lined with aluminum foil and bake until soft, 40 to 45 minutes.

While the squash is baking, heat the oil in a large skillet over moderately high heat. Add the onion and cook, stirring frequently, until golden brown, then add the garlic and cook, stirring, another 2 minutes. Add the ginger, tomatoes, and honey and cook until the sauce begins to simmer. Add the curry powder, rice, and chickpeas and continue to cook, stirring frequently, until the mixture is hot. Stir in the coriander, salt, and pepper and cook 2 minutes more. Remove the skillet from the heat, cover, and let rest 2 to 3 minutes to allow the rice to absorb the liquid. Spoon the mixture into the baked squash and serve immediately.

# Caramelized Onion–Stuffed
# Potato Tart

**Makes** 8 **servings**

Lora: *This makes a great breakfast side dish, a vegetarian entrée, or an accompaniment to roast game, lamb, or beef.*

Max: *If you are serving the tart with meat, try adding some mango chutney to the onions for a sweet-and-spicy touch.*

Salt 2 medium-size Idaho potatoes, peeled and cut in half crosswise

2 tablespoons olive oil

1 medium-size Vidalia or other sweet onion, sliced

1 tablespoon fresh rosemary leaves, chopped

2 tablespoons butter

Preheat the oven to 375°F with the rack set in the upper third but not at the highest position. Bring a small pan of salted water to a rapid boil, add the potatoes, and reduce the heat to a simmer. Cook, uncovered, until slightly cooked but still quite firm and quite undercooked, about 10 minutes. Drain and let cool. When the potatoes have cooled enough to handle, slice them into rounds crosswise, about the thickness of a penny.

Heat the oil in a small skillet, then add the onion and cook over moderate heat, stirring frequently, until golden brown. Coat an 8-inch ovenproof sauté pan or other round ovenproof casserole with butter and sprinkle salt and a pinch of rosemary into the bottom of the pan. Layer the slices of potato into the pan, starting from the center outward, right up the rim of the pan. When the first layer is complete, add a second layer on top. Sprinkle the rosemary on this layer and add slivers of the butter. Fill in the center of the pie with the caramelized onions and the rest of the rosemary. Add a final layer of potatoes to cover the onion filling. Add more butter slivers to the top of the tart, and another pinch of salt.

Place the pan in the preheated oven and bake until the top is browned, about 45 minutes. Remove the pan from the oven and place a plate upside down on top of it. Carefully flip the plate and pan so the plate is right side up, then remove the pan; the tart will remain on the plate. Cut into slices and serve hot or at room temperature.

# Whole Pumpkin Stuffed with
## Curried Vegetable Stew

Makes 8 to 10
servings

*If you're looking for something to wow company (especially those vegetarian friends of yours), this dish makes the most amazing presentation. A whole baked pumpkin holds a savory vegetable stew. You serve both the stew and the pumpkin. Make sure to get a sugar pumpkin—the other kind isn't good to eat. Also, make sure you get a pumpkin that will fit in your oven (when sitting in a baking dish). Bring a tape measure when you go to the farmstand. Depending on the size of your pumpkin, there may be too much stuffing to fit inside. The rest can be baked in a covered, ovenproof dish.*

1 large or 2 medium-size sugar pumpkins (depending on the size of your oven)

Kosher salt

Vegetable oil

2 cloves garlic, minced

1½ tablespoons peeled and minced fresh ginger

1 medium-size bulb fennel, cut into ½-inch-thick slices

1 medium-size red bell pepper, seeded and cut into 2-inch squares

1 yellow bell pepper, seeded and cut in 2-inch squares

2 small eggplants, cut into 2-inch cubes

2 medium-size zucchini, cut into 2-inch lengths

1 pound cauliflower, cut into 2-inch florets

1 pound broccoli, cut into 2-inch florets

2 carrots, cut into 1-inch-thick slices

Preheat the oven to 400°F with the rack set in the upper third of the oven. Line a heavy-duty baking sheet with aluminum foil and lightly coat the foil with nonstick vegetable spray. Use a sharp knife to slice the top(s) off the pumpkin(s) and use a metal spoon to scrape out the seeds and pulp. Remove as much pulp as possible from the seeds, sprinkle the seeds with kosher salt, and spread them in one layer over the prepared pan. Toast until deep golden brown, 12 to 15 minutes, turning them over once during the cooking. Set aside.

Reduce the oven temperature to 350°F and place the rack in the lowest position. Place the pumpkin(s) in a shallow baking/serving dish (they can't be transferred after cooking).

Heat enough oil to cover the bottom of a large skillet over moderate heat. Add the garlic and ginger and cook, stirring, only until light golden brown. Remove from the skillet to a small dish. Add the fresh vegetables to the skillet one at a time in the order in which they are listed and

One 10-ounce package frozen pearl onions, defrosted

One 10-ounce package frozen artichoke hearts, defrosted

One 10-ounce can chickpeas, (garbanzo beans) drained

1 to 1½ teaspoons salt, to your taste

½ teaspoon cayenne pepper

1 teaspoon freshly ground black pepper

1 teaspoon ground coriander

2 teaspoons ground turmeric

2 cups vegetable stock

Cooked rice

cook until softened, 5 to 10 minutes per vegetable, removing them to a very large bowl (you may have to use more than one bowl) before adding the next vegetable and more oil as necessary. Mix the pearl onions, artichoke hearts, chickpeas, salt and pepper, and spices into the cooked vegetables. Spoon the mixture into the pumpkin(s) and add the stock. Place the top(s) back on the pumpkin(s) and bake until the pumpkin is easily pierced with a knife, about 1 hour. Take care not to overcook, or the pumpkin will collapse, making for a huge mess. To serve, scoop the vegetables and some of the inside of the pumpkin over the cooked rice and garnish with toasted pumpkin seeds.

# Variations on a Stuffed Potato Theme

**Makes 1 serving**

*It was hard to stop with just four variations of stuffed baked potatoes. Each ingredient that we thought of (short of chocolate) seemed to fit in better than the last. Once you make our versions, chances are you'll be inspired to create your own. These can be a meal in themselves, or cut in half and served as a starch for two.*

## Anchovy and Olive–Stuffed Potato

1 large Idaho potato (about 12 ounces), scrubbed

2 tablespoons butter

4 anchovy fillets, drained and chopped

3 large green pitted olives, chopped

## Blue Cheese and Bacon–Stuffed Potato

2 ounces Roquefort cheese

1 strip crisp cooked lean bacon, crumbled

Mash the potato pulp with the cheese, then gently mix in the bacon. Proceed as above.

## Garlic Parmesan–Stuffed Potato

2 tablespoons butter

2 cloves garlic, peeled and minced

2 tablespoons freshly ground Parmesan cheese

Heat the butter in a small skillet, add the garlic, and cook over medium heat, stirring, until the garlic turns light golden brown. Mash the potato pulp with the garlic and butter and cheese, and proceed as above.

*Yes, they're salty—but that's why God, in her wisdom, invented beer.*

Preheat the oven to 375°F with the rack set in the center position. Place the potato directly on the oven rack and cook until the skin is crisp and the interior is soft when a small sharp knife is inserted, about 1 hour. Remove the potato from the oven and use a small, sharp knife to slice off the top quarter. Use a teaspoon to hollow most of the potato out (be careful—too much will make it collapse), saving the pulp in a small bowl. Add the butter, anchovies, and olives to the pulp and use a fork to combine the mixture without making it too smooth. Use the teaspoon to refill the cavity, mounding it as necessary. Place the potato in an ovenproof dish, return it to the oven, and bake 10 more minutes. Serve hot.

## Horseradish-Stuffed Potato

1 tablespoon butter

¼ cup heavy cream

1 tablespoon prepared white horseradish

Combine the pulp and all ingredients, and proceed as above.

# Chocolate- and
# Ice Cream–
# Stuffed
# Desserts

# Cassata alla Siciliana

**Makes 8 to 10 servings**

**Lora:** *This elegant chocolate cake from Sicily uses a store-bought pound cake which is stuffed with a chocolate/ricotta mixture, then frosted with a bittersweet-chocolate espresso frosting.*

**Max:** *I like this better after it has sat for at least a day, or overnight in the refrigerator, because the flavors blend and the cake becomes almost mousselike. How about serving this with a glass of grappa?*

**Lora:** *How do you know about grappa?*

## For the frosting

4 ounces semisweet chocolate, chopped (¾ cup)

¾ cup (1½ sticks) unsalted butter, softened

½ cup brewed espresso, or 1 tablespoon instant espresso powder dissolved in ½ cup boiling water

## For the filling

1 pound whole-milk ricotta

¼ cup confectioners' sugar

Finely grated rind of 1 orange

⅓ cup mini–chocolate chips

## To assemble

1 store-bought chocolate or white pound cake (if frozen, defrost before using)

½ cup Grand Marnier or other orange liqueur, or another liqueur of your choice

To make the frosting, in a small bowl set over a pan of gently simmering (not boiling) water, melt the chocolate together with the butter and espresso. Mix to combine completely and then refrigerate, stirring every 15 minutes, until firm.

In either a food processor or a stand mixer or by hand using a whisk, blend together the ricotta, sugar, and orange rind. Fold in the chocolate chips.

Use a serrated knife to cut the pound cake twice horizontally, making 3 equal layers. Place 1 layer on a flat plate and sprinkle half the liqueur over it. Spread half the ricotta mixture on top. Top with the second layer and repeat the process. Top with the third and final layer. Use a narrow cake spatula to frost the top of the cake with the cooled frosting. You may frost the sides as well, or leave the layers exposed. Refrigerate until serving. To serve, cut the cake into thin slices.

# Mole Truffle Torte

Makes **1** nine-inch torte; **10** servings

**Max:** *This is not a "stuffed" recipe in the traditional sense, but it's so unbelievably good, I begged my mother to put it in.*

**Lora:** *His wish is my command. This is an amazing confection—deep, rich flourless chocolate, studded with, believe it or not, chiles. Trust me, there are just enough to light your interest, but not inflame your palate. The figs add body and sweetness. This wonderful dessert, created by Liz Corrado of Albany, New York, was the unanimous first-prize winner in Albany's annual Chocolate Festival.*

2 medium-size ancho chiles

20 dried Black Mission figs, stems removed

⅓ cup firmly packed brown sugar

2 tablespoons pure vanilla extract, divided

1 pound bittersweet (not unsweetened) chocolate—Callebaut is the best

1 cup (2 sticks) unsalted butter

1 tablespoon ground cinnamon

6 large eggs

Preheat the oven to 425°F with the rack set in the center position. Generously coat a 9-inch springform pan with butter. Line the bottom with waxed paper or parchment paper and butter that. Cover the outside of the pan in a double layer of aluminum foil to prevent water from the water pan leaking in and set aside until ready to use.

Place the chiles in the oven for 3 minutes, or until they are just softened. (If left in longer, they will become crisp and unusable.) Remove the stems and seeds.

Place the chiles, figs, brown sugar, and 1 tablespoon of the vanilla in a medium-size saucepan and cover with 1 inch of water. Cook over moderate heat until the figs are soft. Purée the mixture until smooth in a blender or in the work bowl of a food processor fitted with the metal blade; a blender will yield a smoother mixture. You may strain the mixture to remove some of the fig seeds if you like; I like to leave them in. Set aside to cool. Do not chill.

In a large bowl set over simmering (not boiling) water, melt the chocolate and butter together. Do not allow the water to touch the bottom of the bowl. Remove from the heat when almost melted and stir until smooth. Add the remaining tablespoon vanilla and the cinnamon. When cooled to room temperature (do not chill), stir in ¾ cup of the fig mixture. The chocolate will now appear slightly lumpy.

Place the eggs in a medium-size mixing bowl set over very hot water. Stirring constantly to prevent curdling, heat until just warm to the touch. Then transfer to a stand mixer, or use a hand mixer, to beat on medium-high speed until tripled in volume. (If using a hand mixture, mix over warm water to get enough volume.)

Using a rubber spatula, fold one quarter of the eggs into the chocolate mixture until just incorporated. Add the rest of the eggs and fold until no light streaks are evident.

Pour the batter into the prepared pan and set in a large pan filled with about an inch of very hot water. The sides of the large pan must not be higher than the springform pan or the cake will not cook properly. Bake, uncovered, for 5 minutes, then loosely cover with a sheet of buttered aluminum foil and bake another 10 minutes. The cake will appear very loose. Remove the cake from the water and place the pan on a wire rack until cooled to room temperature. Cover tightly with plastic wrap and chill for at least 3 hours.

To unmold, wipe the bottom and sides of the springform with a hot towel. This should soften it enough to remove smoothly. Remove the sides and bottom carefully. Sift the cinnamon over the top and use your fingers to rub it in to get a smooth appearance. Serve at room temperature with unsweetened whipped cream.

# Chocolate Roulade Filled with Chocolate Ice Cream

**Makes 8 to 10 servings**

**Max:** *In our family this is the most-requested birthday cake. The celebrant gets to pick his own flavor of ice cream. For my Bar Mitzvah, my mother made a dozen of these, filled them with whipped cream instead of ice cream, frosted them, and put them end to end. Then she wrote each guest's name on the cake. I think her undertaking was harder than mine.*

**Lora:** *This is an easy do-ahead dessert. You can make the cake and fill it, then freeze it until it's time to serve.*

8 extra-large eggs, at room temperature

1 cup sugar, divided

⅓ cup plus 3 tablespoons unsweetened cocoa powder—not Dutch-process (Hershey's, for example, works well), sifted, divided

2 tablespoons unbleached all-purpose flour

### For the filling

2 pints best-quality ice cream or low-fat frozen yogurt, slightly softened (see below)

### To serve

2 cups store-bought or homemade hot fudge sauce

Preheat the oven to 350°F with the rack set in the center position. Line an 11-by-17-inch heavy-duty jelly-roll pan with parchment paper. Spray the parchment and the sides of the pan lightly with nonstick vegetable spray. Separate the eggs, placing the yolks in a 2-quart mixing bowl and the whites in a metal 2-quart mixing bowl that has been carefully washed with hot water and then dried. With either a large wire whisk or an electric mixer, beat the egg yolks with *half* the sugar until they are thick and light yellow, 15 to 20 minutes by hand, and 6 to 8 minutes with an electric mixer. On slow speed, mix in ⅓ cup of the cocoa and the flour. Wash the beaters or whisk very well with hot water and soap, then dry well. Beat the egg whites with the remaining ½ cup sugar until they hold soft peaks, but not so much that they look stiff and dry.

Scoop one third of the egg whites into the chocolate bowl and use a rubber scraper to mix the two together gently. Then scoop the remaining egg whites onto the chocolate mixture and use the rubber scraper to fold the two together until you can no longer see any traces of white. Pour and scrape the batter into the prepared pan and spread it evenly. Bake until the top looks dry and the sides have pulled away from the pan, 15 to 18 minutes, reversing the position of the pan front to back halfway through the baking time.

Remove the cake from the oven and place the pan on a wire rack. Rinse a clean kitchen towel with water, then wring out as much water as you possibly can—the towel should be barely damp. Cover the cake with the towel and let it rest until the cake is completely cool. Release the edges by cutting around the sides of the pan with a small, sharp knife. Dust the surface of the cake with the remaining 3 tablespoons cocoa. This prevents the plastic wrap from sticking to the cake when the cake is inverted.

Cut two 20-inch lengths of plastic wrap and lay them overlapping on top of the cake so that there is an overflow of several inches on all sides. Place a large baking sheet or lightweight tray on top of the cake and invert both so that the bottom of the jelly-roll pan is on top, and the baking sheet or tray is underneath the cake. Carefully lift off the pan and peel off the parchment paper. Trim the edges of the cake with scissors.

You can soften the ice cream or frozen yogurt either by leaving the containers at room temperature for ½ hour or by microwaving the carton for 15 seconds or so, until the ice cream is slightly softened. Gently spread the ice cream or yogurt to within 1 inch of the cake's borders. Position the cake so the long side is facing you. Use the plastic wrap to help roll the cake away from you, to make a long roll. Cover with the plastic wrap and a layer of aluminum foil. Freeze until ready to serve, at least 2 hours and as long as 3 months.

Remove the roulade from the freezer and use a long, sharp knife to slice it into 1½-or 2-inch-thick slices, laying each on its side on a dessert plate. Drizzle with hot fudge sauce and serve immediately.

# Ice Cream–Stuffed Pound Cake with Raspberry Sauce and Whipped Cream

Makes 8 servings

**Lora:** *Though you can make this using store-bought pound cake, homemade is so much better. We made this cake with vanilla ice cream, then decided any flavor would be great—so use your favorite.*

**Max:** *My favorite is chocolate pound cake stuffed with ginger ice cream. You can easily turn this recipe into a chocolate pound cake by adding two packets of ChocoBake (a liquid chocolate product made by Nestlé) to the batter. If you can't find ChocoBake, use two squares of melted unsweetened baking chocolate.*

### For the pound cake

3 cups unbleached all-purpose flour, measured after sifting

1 teaspoon baking powder

½ teaspoon baking soda

½ teaspoon salt

2 teaspoons lime oil, or finely grated rind of 2 limes

1 cup heavy cream

1½ cups (3 sticks) unsalted butter, softened

One 16-ounce box dark-brown sugar

4 extra-large eggs

### For the raspberry sauce

Two 10-ounce packages frozen raspberries, slightly defrosted, juice reserved

Preheat the oven to 325°F with the rack set in the center position. Generously butter a 10-inch tube pan, dust it with flour, tapping out the excess, and set aside. Sift together the flour, baking powder, baking soda, and salt in a medium-size mixing bowl. Add the lime oil or the rind to the cream and set aside.

In a large mixing bowl, cream the butter with an electric mixer until light. Gradually add the sugar and continue beating until the mixture is very light and fluffy. Reduce the speed to medium and add the eggs one at a time, beating well after each addition. With the mixer on low speed, add one third of the flour, then half of the cream. Add another third of the flour, then the rest of the cream. Finally, add the remaining flour. Mix only until the ingredients are blended. (Overmixing will make for a tough cake.)

One 8-ounce jar good-quality
  seedless raspberry preserves
¼ cup framboise (raspberry
  liqueur; optional)

## To complete
1 pint best-quality ice cream,
  softened
Whipped cream
Fresh raspberries

Spread the batter evenly in the prepared pan, smoothing the top with a rubber spatula. Bake until a cake tester inserted halfway between the side of the pan and the tube comes out clean and dry, about 1 hour. Cool the cake in the pan on a cake rack for 15 minutes, then unmold onto the rack and allow to cool completely.

Place the frozen raspberries, preserves, and framboise (if desired) in the work bowl of a food processor fitted with the metal blade or a blender, and process or blend until smooth. If you wish to make seedless sauce, stir and scrape the mixture through a fine-mesh strainer. Refrigerate until ready to use. Can be frozen up to 6 months.

Use a long, sharp serrated knife to slice the cooled cake horizontally into 3 layers. Spread half the ice cream on the bottom layer and top with the middle layer. Spread this layer with the remaining ice cream and add the top layer. Wrap the cake in aluminum foil and freeze for at least 2 hours. To serve, pour a small pool of raspberry sauce on each plate, cut the cake into vertical slices, and place on the sauce. Add a dollop of whipped cream and some fresh raspberries and serve immediately.

# Chocolate Cream–Filled Chocolate Cupcakes

**Makes 24 cupcakes**

**Lora:** *These cupcakes are light chocolate in color and light in texture as well. They are filled with a walnut-sized blob of rich chocolate cream. Besides two standard-size cupcake or muffin tins, and fluted paper cupcake-pan liners, you will need a standard star piping tip (available in cookware shops and many department stores).*

**Max:** *Be sure to have a couple of gallons of cold milk for the kids and guests that you serve the cupcakes to.*

1 cup whole milk

6 tablespoons (¾ stick) butter, cut into 6 pieces

3 ounces unsweetened baking chocolate, chopped into small pieces

3 extra-large eggs

1½ cups granulated sugar

2 cups all-purpose flour

2 teaspoons baking powder

½ teaspoon salt

## For the filling

1 cup heavy cream

10 ounces semisweet or bittersweet chocolate, chopped into small pieces

½ cup confectioners' sugar

Preheat the oven to 350°F with the racks positioned so the oven is divided into thirds. Lightly spray the top of two 12-hole cupcake or muffin pans with nonstick vegetable spray (or wipe with vegetable oil). Line the holes with fluted-paper or foil cupcake holders.

Place the milk, butter, and chocolate in a small saucepan over moderate heat and stir frequently until the butter and chocolate melt. Do not allow the milk to boil. The mixture will be speckled—that's fine. Remove the pan from the heat and allow to cool slightly while you prepare the batter.

Place the eggs and granulated sugar in a deep 2-quart metal bowl. Using a whisk or an electric mixer, beat them together until the mixture is thick and yellow, 6 to 8 minutes by hand or 5 minutes with an electric mixer.

Place a mesh strainer over the egg mixture and add the flour, baking powder, and salt. Agitate the strainer to sift the dry ingredients over the egg mixture. Mix gently by hand or machine just until you can no longer see any flour. Take care not to overmix, for this will make the cupcakes tough.

Dribble in the chocolate/butter mixture while stirring gently either by hand or with the electric mixer. Mix, scraping down the sides and bottom of the bowl with a rubber scraper, only until the batter is smooth. It will still appear lightly speckled.

Fill each cupcake liner three-quarters full (there should be about ¼ inch of paper showing around the edge). Place the tins in the oven and set the timer for 8 minutes. At the end of this time, reverse the pans, rack to rack and front to back. Bake until the tops are gently rounded and appear spongy and a cake tester or toothpick inserted in the center comes out clean, another 8 to 10 minutes. Cool the cupcakes in the tins for 10 minutes, then remove them to a wire rack to cool completely before filling and frosting.

To make the filling, place the cream in a 1-quart saucepan and set it over moderate heat. When small bubbles form around the edge of the pan, remove it from the heat and add the chocolate. Stir gently with a wire whisk until the chocolate melts and the mixture is smooth. (You can also make this in a food processor fitted with the metal blade, by placing the pieces of chocolate in the work bowl and adding the hot cream. Cover and process until the mixture is smooth, 10 to 15 seconds.) Allow the mixture to cool to warm at room temperature. This will take several hours, depending on the temperature of your kitchen.

Select a quart-size heavy-duty zippered-top plastic bag. Use scissors to snip ¼ inch off one of the bottom corners. Slip the piping tip inside the bag so that the small end sticks out through the opening you have made. When the chocolate mixture is the consistency of mashed potatoes, spoon about half of it into the plastic bag. Seal the bag, squeezing as much air out as possible.

Use a small knife to cut a slit 1¼ inches deep and about 1¼ inches wide in the top of each cupcake. Insert the piping tube into each slit, then gently but firmly squeeze about 1 rounded tablespoon of filling into the cupcake and lift the tip to create a small rosette on the top. Sift a dusting of confectioners' sugar over the tops of the cupcakes and store at room temperature until ready to serve.

# Chocolate-Filled Brioches

Makes **12** large brioches or **24** mini-brioches

**Lora:** *Tender, rich egg bread encases bits of bittersweet chocolate in this heavenly recipe. It's essential to give the dough a long rise in the refrigerator to develop the flavor and give it the right consistency for shaping. You can substitute an equal amount of Lora Brody's Dough Relaxer (available from the* King Arthur Flour Baker's Catalogue, 800-827-6836*) for the nonfat dry milk to make the dough easy to roll.*

**Max:** *If you can find Gianduja, which is a milk chocolate made with ground hazelnuts, try it instead of the dark chocolate. Gianduja is available in most Italian food stores and many gourmet stores as well.*

### For the brioche dough

1 tablespoon dry yeast

3 tablespoons sugar

3 tablespoons nonfat dry milk

3 tablespoons Lora Brody's Dough Relaxer (optional for a richer, softer brioche)

1½ teaspoons salt

3¼ cups all-purpose flour

1 cup (2 sticks) unsalted butter, melted and slightly cooled

3 extra-large eggs

¼ to ⅓ cup warm water, if needed

### To complete and bake the brioches

2 to 3 tablespoons butter, softened

Twelve 1-ounce chunks best-quality bittersweet chocolate

1 large egg yolk mixed with ¼ cup heavy cream

Coarse sugar

This dough will be extremely sticky at first, then slightly less so as the kneading progresses. Some of it will continue to stick to the bottom of the pan or work bowl—don't be tempted to add more flour. It is quite a loose dough, but will firm up when chilled. The dough should be very wet.

*For the food processor:* Place the dry ingredients for the dough in the work bowl of a food processor fitted with the plastic blade. With the machine running, add the butter and eggs and process for 40 seconds after the liquid is absorbed. The dough should be extremely wet and may not even form a ball. Add the water if needed. Allow the dough to rest for 10 minutes, then process another 40 seconds. With the cover on the machine, allow the dough to rise until doubled in bulk. *For the stand mixer:* Place all the ingredients, including the water, in the mixing bowl of a stand mixer fitted with the dough hook. Knead on low speed until the liquid is absorbed, then on medium speed until a very sticky dough is achieved, 5 to 7 minutes. Cover and let rest for 20 minutes, then knead until the dough is soft and supple but still on the wet side, another 7 to 8 minutes. *For the bread machine:* Place all the ingredients, including the water, in the pan, program for Dough, and press Start.

No matter what method is used, once the dough has risen, place it in a heavy-duty zippered-top plastic bag and refrigerate for at least 24 hours, but no longer than 36 hours.

Use the softened butter to grease very generously 12 mini-brioche tins (with approximately 2½-inch openings). Roll the chilled dough out into a rough 14-inch circle. Cut the dough with a round cookie cutter slightly larger that the opening of the brioche mold, about 3½ inches. (You may need to reroll the scraps of dough to get 12 circles.) Place a chunk of chocolate in the center of each circle, gather the edges up, and pinch them together to make a ball. Place the balls as you make them seam side down in the prepared tins. Brush with the egg wash and sprinkle generously with coarse sugar. Place the tins on a heavy-duty baking sheet and set in a warm, draft-free place to rise until doubled in size.

Preheat the oven to 425°F with the rack set in the lower third but not at the lowest position of the oven. Bake the brioches for 5 minutes at 425°F, then reduce the oven temperature to 375°F and bake an additional 10 to 12 minutes. If the tops turn very brown before the baking time is up, cover loosely with a sheet of aluminum foil. The internal temperature should register 190° to 200°F on an instant-read thermometer. Cool the brioches for at least 15 minutes before serving hot, or cool completely to room temperature.

# Ice-Cream Sandwiches

Makes 8 sandwiches

**Lora:** *You can forget about those skinny, cardboard-tasting ice-cream sandwiches you buy in the supermarket. Premium ice cream (in the flavor of your choice, of course) is stuffed between two homemade chewy chocolate chocolate-chunk cookies. If you're in a real hurry, you can buy the cookies; just make sure they're the soft kind, so they don't break when you put the sandwich together.*

**Max:** *You can use frozen yogurt instead of ice cream. And your favorite oatmeal-raisin cookie recipe instead of chocolate-chip. I like oatmeal raisin cookies stuffed with Ben & Jerry's Cherry Garcia ice cream. Try rolling the edges of the ice cream in shaved chocolate after you fill the sandwiches.*

## For the cookies

2 ounces unsweetened baking chocolate, chopped

2 cups all-purpose flour, measured after sifting

1 teaspoon baking powder

½ teaspoon salt

1 cup firmly packed light-brown sugar

½ cup (1 stick) butter, softened

1 large egg

1 cup whole milk

1½ teaspoons pure vanilla extract

8 ounces semisweet chocolate, cut into ¼ inch chunks (1⅔ cups)

## To make the ice-cream sandwiches

1½ pints premium ice cream, very slightly softened

Preheat the oven to 350°F with the rack set in the center position. Grease 2 heavy-duty baking sheets or line them with parchment paper. Melt the unsweetened chocolate either in the microwave or in the top of a double boiler set over gently simmering (not boiling) water. Set aside to cool slightly. Sift the flour, baking powder, and salt together into a medium-size mixing bowl. In a large mixing bowl, cream the sugar and butter together until light and fluffy. Add the egg, milk, and vanilla, and mix well to combine. Stir in the melted chocolate, then the flour, and finally the chocolate chunks.

Use a large spoon or an ice-cream scoop to form sixteen 2-inch balls from the dough and place them 2½ inches apart on the prepared baking sheets. These cookies will be baked one sheet at a time for 15 minutes. As soon as the cookies are removed from the oven, smack the baking sheet sharply on the counter—this will collapse the cookies and make them soft. Repeat with the other sheet. Cool completely on wire racks.

Cut eight 10-inch-square pieces of plastic wrap. Place one cookie on each square. Use an ice-cream scoop to place a generous scoop of ice cream in the center of the cookie, then top with another cookie, pressing down on the top lightly before pulling up the plastic wrap around the cookie to enclose it completely. Press down a bit more so that the ice cream flows to the edge of the cookie. Place each sandwich in the freezer as you form it. Freeze for at least 1 hour or as long as several weeks.

# White and Dark Chocolate Cannoli

Makes **12** cannoli

**Max:** *Dipping both ends of a cannoli shell in melted chocolate, then filling it with a mixture of ricotta and cream cheese sweetened with white chocolate makes for a visually beautiful dessert. The combination of tastes and textures is amazing. You can buy cannoli shells in most Italian markets and many grocery stores.*

**Lora:** *For the best taste, it's essential to buy "real" white chocolate, made with cocoa butter, not palm-kernel or coconut oil. Read the label carefully.*

12 ounces semisweet chocolate chips

12 cannoli shells

## For the filling

1½ cups (¾ pound) whole-milk ricotta cheese

One 8-ounce package cream cheese, softened

½ cup confectioners' sugar, sifted

¼ teaspoon pure vanilla extract

2 tablespoons grated orange rind

3 ounces white chocolate, finely chopped (see Headnote)

2 tablespoons Grand Marnier or other orange liqueur

Melt the chocolate chips, either in the microwave oven, or in a double boiler over gently simmering (not boiling) water. Stir until smooth, then dip the ends of the cannoli shells in the chocolate to cover by about ¼ inch at each end. Set on waxed-paper– or parchment-paper–lined baking sheets to harden at room temperature.

Cream the ricotta cheese and cream cheese together in a large mixing bowl with a wooden spoon until smooth. Mix in the confectioners' sugar, vanilla, orange rind, white chocolate, and Grand Marnier. Refrigerate the filling in a covered bowl for at least 4 hours.

Just before serving, use a pastry bag fitted with a large star tip to pipe a generous rosette of the filling into each end of the cannoli shells. Sprinkle with more confectioners' sugar and serve immediately.

# Fruit-Filled, Filled Fruit, and a Couple of Sweet Extras

# Baked Apples Stuffed with Mascarpone and Dried Apples

*Granny Smith apples are wonderful in this recipe, which combines the tartness of the fresh apples, the sweetness of dried apples, and the creamy tang of mascarpone, which is a sweet, soft Italian cream cheese available in specialty food shops and many Italian markets. Apple brandy or Calvados gives this fall dish the perfect finish. You may substitute apple cider, if you wish.*

6 very large sturdy, flavorful apples, such as Granny Smith

⅔ cup dried apples, cut into 1-inch pieces (kitchen scissors work well for this)

½ cup apple brandy, Calvados, or apple cider

8 ounces mascarpone (or substitute cream cheese)

½ cup firmly packed dark-brown sugar

Preheat the oven to 350°F with the rack set in the center position. Remove a 1-inch ring of peel if necessary to make the apples stand upright. Use a grapefruit spoon to scoop out a pocket 1½ inches wide by 2½ inches deep in the center of each apple. Remove as much of the core and seeds as possible, and place the apples in a shallow baking dish.

Place the dried apples and brandy or cider in a small saucepan over moderate heat. Allow the mixture to simmer gently, uncovered, stirring occasionally, until the apples are softened and have absorbed most of the liquid, 6 to 8 minutes. Off the heat, stir in the mascarpone and brown sugar. Gently spoon this mixture into the centers of the apples. Add 1 inch of water to the baking dish and bake until the apples are tender when pierced with a sharp knife, about 25 to 30 minutes.

Serve hot, warm, or at room temperature, spooning any liquid in the dish over the apples.

# Cranberry-Apple Turnovers

**Makes 8 turnovers**

**Max:** *We are lucky to live in Massachusetts, where fresh cranberries are readily available from late summer through early winter. If you can't find fresh, frozen are fine in this light, fruit-filled pastry.*

1 package active dry yeast

1 cup lukewarm milk (98° to 110°F)

3 tablespoons butter, melted, or vegetable oil

3 tablespoons honey

3 cups unbleached all-purpose flour

1 teaspoon salt

¾ cup cranberries, picked over and rinsed

2 large Granny Smith apples, cored, peeled, and thinly sliced

½ cup water

¼ cup dried currants

1 cup pure maple syrup, divided

3 tablespoons cornstarch

Juice and finely grated rind of 1 lemon

½ teaspoon ground cinnamon

In a bread machine or the work bowl of a food processor fitted with the plastic blade, combine the yeast, milk, oil or butter, honey, flour, and salt. Knead or process until a smooth, supple ball of dough has formed. Allow the dough to rise until doubled in bulk (you can leave it in the food processor for this, or program for Knead and First Rise in the bread machine), then punch the dough down and let it rest, covered, for 10 minutes before proceeding.

In a large saucepan over moderately high heat, simmer the cranberries, apples, water, and currants together, covered, until the cranberries pop. In a small mixing bowl, combine ⅔ cup of the maple syrup, the cornstarch, lemon juice, and rind and cinnamon. Uncover the saucepan and add the maple-syrup mixture to the cooking cranberries. Stir well. Heat, stirring constantly, until thickened. Remove from the heat and let cool for 15 minutes.

Preheat the oven to 375°F. Lightly oil a large heavy-duty baking sheet. Divide the dough evenly into 8 balls. Roll each into a 5-inch circle on a floured work surface. Place equal amounts of the cranberry filling in the center of each circle. Lightly dampen the edges of the circle with water and fold the edges in to form a turnover, pressing with the tines of a fork to seal.

In a small saucepan over high heat, bring the remaining ⅓ cup maple syrup to a boil and cook for 3 to 4 minutes. Remove from the heat and brush the tops of the turnovers with it. Place the turnovers on the prepared baking sheet and bake until browned, about 20 minutes. Let cool slightly before serving.

# Apple-Stuffed Strudel

*Makes* **8** *servings*

**Lora:** *Working with phyllo dough is something that gets easier with practice. This lovely dessert will make the practice worthwhile.*

**Max:** *When working with phyllo dough, I find it best to leave the dough refrigerated while I prepare all of the other ingredients in the recipe, then keep the dough covered with plastic wrap reaching under to get sheets as needed while I assemble the strudel.*

4 large Granny Smith apples, cored, peeled, and finely chopped

½ cup sugar

1 teaspoon ground cinnamon

¾ cup seedless raisins

¼ cup blanched slivered almonds

½ cup (1 stick) unsalted butter, melted, divided

4 sheets frozen phyllo dough, defrosted

¼ cup, vegetable oil

2 tablespoons plain dried bread crumbs.

Mix the apples together with the sugar, cinnamon, raisins, almonds, and 2 tablespoons of the melted butter.

Unwrap the phyllo dough and keep the sheets between 2 dampened tea towels. Combine the oil and remaining butter. Place a sheet of dough on a third tea towel, brush it with the butter/oil mixture, and sprinkle with 1½ teaspoons of the bread crumbs. Place a second sheet of phyllo on top of the first, brush with butter, and sprinkle with crumbs. Repeat with the remaining 2 sheets of phyllo.

Spread the apple filling along one long side of the dough to within 2 inches of each edge. The filling should be in a mounded row about 3 inches wide. Fold the long side over once to cover the filling, then fold in edges. Continue to roll lengthwise, like a jelly roll, using the towel to help.

Preheat the oven to 400°F with the rack set in the center position. Lightly butter a heavy-duty baking sheet. Brush the roll with butter and place it seam side down on the prepared baking sheet. Bake until golden, 20 to 25 minutes. Remove from the oven and lightly score the top into 1½-inch-thick slices with a sharp knife. Cool, cut into slices, and serve warm or at room temperature.

# Plum-Stuffed Focaccia

Makes 10 wedges

**Lora:** *This rich, moist, sweet dough is formed into a flat disk, then studded with Italian-plum halves, topped with egg glaze, and sprinkled with coarse sugar. This beautiful creation makes the ultimate brunch showpiece.*

**Max:** *If Italian plums aren't in season, you can soften dried berries (strawberries, cranberries, blueberries) or dried cherries in some orange juice and use them instead.*

## For the dough

1 tablespoon active dry yeast

½ cup milk, heated to 120°F

½ cup granulated sugar, divided

¼ cup (½ stick) unsalted butter, very soft

2 extra-large eggs

1 teaspoon lime oil, or finely grated rind of 2 limes

½ teaspoon salt

½ cup yellow cornmeal

3 cups all-purpose flour

## To complete the focaccia

1½ tablespoons butter, softened

8 Italian (prune) plums, cut into halves, pits removed

1 large egg mixed with 1 tablespoon water

1 to 2 tablespoons coarse sugar

Place the yeast, milk, and 1 teaspoon of the granulated sugar in a large mixing bowl and stir to dissolve the yeast. When the mixture begins to foam, add the remaining dough ingredients, including the remaining sugar, and mix with your hands to combine. Turn the mixture out onto a lightly floured work surface and knead for 5 to 8 minutes, until you have a smooth, soft ball, adding a small amount of flour if necessary to keep the dough from sticking to the work surface. Form the dough into a ball and place it in a well-oiled bowl, cover with plastic wrap, and set in a warm, draft-free place to rise until doubled in bulk, about 1 hour. You can complete this step up to a day in advance and keep in the refrigerator.

Use the 1½ tablespoons softened butter to grease a heavy-duty baking sheet or pizza round. Use your hands to form the dough into an 11-inch disk and place it on the prepared sheet. Use your finger to poke holes 1½ inches apart over the entire surface of the dough and insert a plum half, cut side up, into each hole. You'll have to poke rather aggressively to push the fruit into the dough—it doesn't have to disappear, but should rest in a small indentation. Continue until the top of the focaccia is covered with plums. Brush the top with the egg glaze. Top with a generous sprinkling of coarse sugar.

Let the focaccia rise in a warm, draft-free place for 30 minutes, then preheat the oven to 400°F with the rack set in the center position. Bake for 15 minutes at 400°F, then reduce the oven temperature to 350°F, covering the focaccia with aluminum foil if it is getting very brown. Bake until the crust is deep golden brown and the bottom of the focaccia is dry, about another 15 minutes. Cool for 10 minutes before cutting into wedges, and serve hot or warm.

# Apricot-Filled Crêpes

Makes 4 servings

*These delicate, melt-in-your-mouth morsels are in the finest tradition of Hungarian desserts. You can make the crêpes the day before, stack them between sheets of waxed paper or plastic wrap, then assemble the dessert up to three hours before you plan to warm and serve them. Be sure to buy the finest apricot preserves—it makes an important taste difference.*

## For the crêpes

¾ cup unbleached all-purpose flour, measured after sifting

2 tablespoons sugar

¼ teaspoon salt

1 extra-large egg plus 1 extra-large egg yolk

1½ cups whole milk, divided

1 tablespoon butter, melted

2 to 3 tablespoons butter for cooking the crêpes

## To assemble

1½ cups (12 ounces) best-quality apricot preserves

3 tablespoons unsalted butter

¼ cup amaretto, apricot brandy, or orange juice

½ cup finely chopped walnuts

Place the flour, sugar, salt, egg, egg yolk, 1 cup of the milk, and the melted butter in the work bowl of a blender or food processor fitted with the metal blade. Process for 30 seconds, then add the remaining ½ cup milk. Scrape down the sides and process until the milk is completely incorporated and there are no visible lumps, about another 15 seconds. Refrigerate for at least 2 hours before making the crêpes.

Heat 1 tablespoon of the butter in a 6-inch crêpe or omelet pan over moderate heat. When it begins to sizzle, swirl the butter around in the pan so that the entire surface is coated. Pour off any excess butter. Add a scant ¼ cup of the batter to the pan, lift the pan from the burner, and tilt it so the batter coats the bottom and halfway up the sides of the pan. Don't worry about making a perfect circle—you can trim the crêpe later. Cook until the underside is lightly browned, about 90 seconds; don't worry if it's not evenly colored. Use a spatula to flip the crêpe over and cook the other side for an additional 30 seconds. Continue cooking the crêpes, adding more butter as necessary to keep them from sticking to the pan. Stack the crêpes between layers of waxed paper. Cover with plastic wrap and refrigerate until ready to assemble the dessert.

To assemble, spread 2 to 3 tablespoons of the preserves over the bottom of each crêpe. Roll the crêpes up loosely. Heat the unsalted butter together with the amaretto in a 10-to 12-inch sauté pan over moderate heat. When the mixture begins to simmer, add the filled crêpes seam side down and cook, spooning some of the cooking liquid over the tops, until the insides are hot when tested with a small sharp knife, 4 to 5 minutes. Sprinkle with the walnuts and serve immediately.

# Rum Tums

**Makes 12 biscuits**

*As our pal P. J. Hamel says, "When you use sweet butter, heavy cream, rum, and sugar in a recipe, you can't possibly go wrong." These sweet biscuits were P. J.'s invention. We tested them one perfectly glorious August afternoon, then sat out on the deck and ate them with a bottle of really good Chardonnay—heaven.*

## For the dough

½ cup (1 stick) butter

2 cups unbleached all-purpose flour

1 tablespoon sugar

2½ teaspoons baking powder

½ teaspoon salt

1 cup heavy cream

## To complete

12 sugar cubes (white or unrefined)

¼ cup rum

1 large egg yolk mixed with 2 tablespoons whole milk or cream

2 tablespoons coarse sugar

⅛ teaspoon grated nutmeg

Preheat the oven to 425°F with the rack set in the center position. Line a heavy-duty baking sheet with parchment paper. Place the butter and dry ingredients for the dough in the work bowl of a food processor fitted with the plastic blade and pulse until the mixture resembles fine crumbs. With the processor running, dribble in the cream until a soft ball forms; do not overmix, or the biscuits will be tough. To mix by hand, use a pastry cutter or 2 forks to work the butter into the dry ingredients until the mixture resembles coarse crumbs. Add the cream and mix with your hands until the dough forms a rough ball. Remove the dough to a very lightly floured counter and knead 4 to 6 times to make a smooth ball. Flatten the dough and roll or pat it out into a 6-by-3-inch rectangle ¾ inch thick.

Cut the dough into 12 squares and use your thumb to poke an indentation in the center of each one. Briefly soak the sugar cubes in the rum, then place one in each indentation, pushing down slightly to anchor it. It should be level with the surface. Brush the top with the egg glaze. Combine the coarse sugar and nutmeg and sprinkle this generously over the top of each biscuit. Place the biscuits at least 2 inches apart on the prepared baking sheet and bake until the tops are golden brown, 20 to 30 minutes. Cool for 10 minutes before serving. Serve hot, warm, or at room temperature. These are best eaten fresh and should not be refrigerated.

# Sour Cherry–Filled Cream Tart

Makes **1** nine-inch tart; **8** servings

**Lora:** *You can find canned pitted sour cherries in the supermarket and gourmet shops. This light, buttery streusel-topped pastry is perfect for brunch or tea.*

**Max:** *Even if the can or jar says "pitted," make sure to check. That used to be my job when Mom made this dessert. Sure enough, I'd find at least two or three pits every time.*

## For the dough

1 teaspoon active dry yeast

1½ cups unbleached all-purpose flour

2 tablespoons firmly packed dark-brown sugar

½ teaspoon salt

½ cup water

1 tablespoon grated lemon zest

2 tablespoons butter, softened

1 large egg yolk

## For the filling

One 8-ounce package cream cheese, very soft

Juice and finely grated zest of 1 lemon

3 tablespoons granulated sugar

2 large egg yolks

1 teaspoon pure vanilla extract

1½ cups canned pitted sour cherries, drained

## For the streusel

2 tablespoons unsalted butter

2 tablespoons firmly packed dark-brown sugar

2 tablespoons all-purpose flour

To make the dough, place the yeast, flour, brown sugar, and salt in a food processor fitted with the plastic blade. Process just to blend, then, with the machine turned off, add the water, zest, butter, and egg yolk. Process for 40 to 60 seconds. The dough should be very soft and may not even form a ball. Allow the dough to rest in the processor with the cover on for 10 minutes, then process another 40 seconds. With the cover on the machine, allow the dough to rise until doubled in bulk, 40 to 60 minutes. Meanwhile, prepare the filling and streusel topping.

To make the filling, place the cream cheese, lemon juice, and zest, and granulated sugar in a medium-size mixing bowl and use a wooden spoon to cream until smooth. Add the egg yolks and vanilla and mix very well. Refrigerate the filling until you are ready to assemble.

To make the streusel, in a small mixing bowl, use 2 knives or a pastry cutter to cut the butter into the brown sugar, flour, and cinnamon to make coarse crumbs. Stir in the oats and nuts.

To assemble the tart, preheat the oven to 400°F with the rack set in the center position. Lightly grease a 9-inch fluted tart pan with a removable bottom. Place the pan on

1 teaspoon ground cinnamon

2 tablespoons old-fashioned rolled oats, not instant

⅓ cup coarsely chopped walnuts

a baking sheet to make it easier to get it in and out of the oven and to prevent oven spills.

On a lightly floured work surface, roll the dough into a 10-inch circle. Line the tart pan with the dough, taking care not to stretch it so much as pat it into place. Place spoonfuls of the cream-cheese filling over the tart and use a rubber spatula or the back of a spoon to spread it out evenly. Scatter the cherries on top of the filling and sprinkle the streusel over that. Bake the tart for 20 minutes at 400°F, then lower the oven temperature to 350°F and bake until the top and crust are golden brown, another 10 to 12 minutes. Cool in the pan for 10 minutes before removing the sides. Serve warm or at room temperature.

# Millie's Hamantaschen

Makes 24 cookies

**Max:** *My grandmother Millie Apter of Hartford, Connecticut, sets the gold standard when it comes to baking. These cookies are her specialty.*

**Lora:** *These triangular-shaped cookies get their name from the tricorner hat worn by that depraved villain Haman, who set out to rid Persia of Jews but in fact ended up being hanged himself, thanks to the brave Queen Esther.*

*These plum pockets are traditionally filled with lekvar, which is a thick fruit butter made with prunes or apricots, or a filling made with poppy seeds, apples, raisins, and almonds. Lekvar is available in specialty food stores and in the preserves section of many supermarkets. The poppy seed filling comes in cans, but the homemade kind is so much better (recipe for homemade poppy seed filling follows).*

## For the dough
3½ cups all-purpose flour
2 teaspoons baking powder
1 teaspoon baking soda
1 scant teaspoon salt
¾ cup sugar
¾ cup vegetable oil
3 large eggs plus 1 large egg white (reserve the yolk for the egg wash)
Finely grated rind of 1 lemon
3 tablespoons fresh lemon juice
1 teaspoon pure vanilla extract

## To form the cookies
3 tablespoons vegetable oil

Sift the flour, baking powder, baking soda, and salt together in a large mixing bowl. Add the remaining dough ingredients and mix either by hand or with an electric mixer until the dough is smooth. Remove it to a floured work surface.

Line a heavy-duty baking sheet with parchment or spray it with nonstick vegetable spray. Divide the dough into 2 equal pieces and roll out to ¼-inch thickness. Using a 4-inch cookie cutter or wide glass, cut out 10 circles. Brush the circles with a light coating of oil and place 1 generous tablespoon of filling in the center of each. Imagine the circle as a triangle, and bring three of the "sides" up to meet in the center, forming a Y-shaped seam. Pinch the edges together to seal (some of the filling will seep out during baking). Place

1½ cups filling—either commercially prepared prune or apricot lekvar, or the Poppy Seed Filling below

1 large egg yolk mixed with 2 tablespoons milk

the cookies on the prepared baking sheet 2 inches apart. Repeat with the remaining dough and filling.

Preheat the oven to 350°F with the rack set in the center position. Brush the tops of the cookies with the egg wash and bake until deep golden brown, 15 to 18 minutes. Cool on a wire rack before enjoying.

## Poppy Seed Filling (optional)

1 large Granny Smith apple, cored and peeled

1 cup poppy seeds

1 cup whole milk

2 tablespoons butter

2 tablespoons honey

½ cup chopped almonds

¼ cup raisins

Finely grated rind of 1 lemon

¼ cup sugar

Grate the apple, either by hand or in the blender or food processor, and set aside. Place the poppy seeds in a blender or food processor and blend or process until they form a thick, crumbly paste. Add the remaining ingredients except the apple, and process or blend until smooth. Place the mixture in a heavy-bottomed saucepan and bring to a boil. Reduce the heat to low and continue cooking, stirring frequently, until the mixture is thick. Cool, then stir in the grated apple.

# S'mores

Makes **18**
S'mores

**Lora:** *Remember s'mores from camp days? Toast a marshmallow till it's black, stick it in between two graham crackers with a piece of Hershey bar, and try to eat it while it's still hot? S'mores are even better when you make the marshmallows and graham crackers from scratch.*

*The graham-cracker recipe was created by P. J. Hamel. This recipe appeared in my book* Desserts from Your Bread Machine: Perfect Every Time *(William Morrow, 1993). The taste will spoil you—you'll never want store-bought again! You can order King Arthur White Wheat Flour from the* King Arthur Flour Baker's Catalogue—800-827-6836—*or find it in a store near you.*

**Max:** *This recipe also calls for an abundant supply of paper towels for the cleaning of the kids after they eat these sloppy sweets.*

## For the marshmallows (makes 20)

Solid vegetable shortening (such as Crisco) for preparing the pan

⅓ cornstarch combined with

⅓ cup granulated sugar for preparing the pan

1 cup cold water, divided

3 tablespoons unflavored gelatin

2 cups superfine sugar

¾ cup light corn syrup

1 tablespoon vanilla extract, or other flavor extract if desired

Confectioners' sugar (for coating the marshmallows)

*A heavy-duty mixer fitted with a whip attachment is required to make these exceptional treats. While this recipe calls for vanilla extract, I've made marshmallows with both mint and orange extracts (both go well with chocolate).*

Coat a 9-inch square pan with 2-inch sides with shortening, then sprinkle on the cornstarch/sugar mixture, tilting the pan to coat all sides and bottom very well. Knock out the excess mixture. Place ½ cup of the water in the large bowl of a heavy-duty mixer fitted with the wire whip or beater attachment. Sprinkle the gelatin over the surface of the water and set aside.

Place the superfine sugar, corn syrup, and remaining ½ cup of water in a heavy-bottomed 1½-quart saucepan set over moderate heat. Stir with a whisk until the sugar dissolves and the

### For the graham crackers (makes 5 to 6 dozen)

1½ cups whole-wheat pastry flour or White Wheat Flour (see Headnote)

1½ cups unbleached all-purpose flour

1½ teaspoons salt

1½ teaspoons baking powder

6 tablespoons (¾ stick) unsalted butter, softened and cut into pieces

1 cup firmly packed dark-brown sugar

½ cup milk plus up to an additional ¼ cup, to make a soft but workable dough

### To complete the graham crackers

1 tablespoon ground cinnamon

¾ cup granulated sugar

### To make the s'mores

Seventy-two 1½-inch squares best-quality bittersweet or milk chocolate (depending on your preference)

36 graham crackers

18 marshmallows

mixture comes to a simmer. Use a pastry brush or dampened dish towel to wipe any sugar crystals from the sides of the pan. Raise the heat to high, insert a candy thermometer, and let the syrup boil without stirring until the temperature reaches 240°F. Remove the pan from the heat and set aside.

With a heavy-duty mixer fitted with the whip attachment on medium speed, add the sugar syrup slowly to the gelatin mixture. When all the syrup has been added, increase the mixer speed to high and beat until the mixture has cooled to lukewarm, and is extremely thick, about 15 minutes. Add the vanilla at the end of the beating time.

Pour and scrape the marshmallow mixture into the prepared pan, smoothing the top with a rubber scraper. Let stand, *uncovered, at room temperature* at least 12 hours, or as long as 24 hours.

Sift the confectioners' sugar onto a work surface to cover an area slightly larger than the pan. Invert the pan onto the prepared surface and, if necessary, use a metal spatula to help loosen and then unmold the marshmallows. Dust off any excess cornstarch. Strain a generous amount of confectioners' sugar over the top to cover completely.

Spray a long thin, sharp knife with nonstick vegetable spray, or wipe it with vegetable oil. Cut the marshmallows into 20 pieces (4 cuts on one side and 5 on the adjacent side). Roll the cut sides of each marshmallow in confectioners' sugar; shake off the excess and store in a tightly covered container (a heavy-duty zippered-top bag is good for this) at room temperature for several weeks.

*continued*

Place all the graham-cracker ingredients except cinnamon and granulated sugar in a bread machine or in the work bowl of an electric mixer. Knead or mix only until the dough forms into a smooth, supple ball. Remove the dough from the machine or mixer and cover with plastic wrap. Refrigerate for 30 minutes.

Preheat the oven to 400°F with the rack set in the center position. Lightly grease several heavy-duty baking sheets. Divide the dough into 4 pieces. Working with one piece at a time (keeping the rest refrigerated) on a lightly floured work surface, roll out into a rough rectangle 1/16 inch thick. Make sure the dough doesn't stick to the surface as you start to roll it out; if it does, sprinkle with additional flour.

Using a pastry cutter, rolling pizza cutter, bench knife, or knife, divide the rectangle into 3-inch squares. Use a metal spatula to transfer the squares to the prepared sheets, placing them close together (they won't spread). Repeat with the remaining pieces of dough, refrigerating the already rolled-out dough.

Mix the cinnamon and sugar together and generously sprinkle each square with it. Bake the sheets one at a time until golden brown, 10 to 12 minutes. Remove the graham crackers from the pan and cool completely on a wire rack. You can store in a covered container for several weeks.

To make the s'mores, lay a graham cracker out and place a square of chocolate on top of it. Over a grill or wood or gas fire, toast a marshmallow until golden brown and just crisp. Place the hot marshmallow on top of the graham-cracker/chocolate-square and top with another piece of chocolate and another graham cracker. Squish slightly and eat immediately. Repeat with the remaining graham crackers, chocolate, and marshmallows.

# Rugelach

**Makes 4 dozen**

Max's *maternal grandmother (the famous Millie of* Bread Machine Baking—Perfect Every Time) *is indisputably the world's best rugelach maker. This is her special recipe for those tender snail cookies stuffed with tart apricots and walnuts. Bet you can't eat just one! My Dough Relaxer is available in gourmet stores and many supermarkets.*

## For the dough

2 cups all-purpose flour, measured after sifting

1 teaspoon salt

1 tablespoon Lora Brody's Dough Relaxer (optional), to make the dough easier to roll

1 cup (2 sticks) unsalted butter, softened

One 8-ounce package cream cheese, softened

¼ cup granulated sugar

2 teaspoons pure vanilla extract

## For the filling

1 cup granulated sugar

½ cup firmly packed dark-brown sugar

1 teaspoon ground cinnamon

1½ cups golden raisins

1½ cups coarsely chopped walnuts

## To assemble

One 12-ounce jar (1½ cups) apricot preserves, gently heated

¼ cup milk

2 tablespoons granulated sugar mixed with 1 teaspoon ground cinnamon

To make the dough, sift together the flour, salt, and Dough Relaxer (if desired) in a medium-size mixing bowl. Either by hand, with an electric mixer, or in the work bowl of a food processor fitted with the plastic blade, cream the butter and cream cheese together until smooth. Mix in the sugar and vanilla. Mix in the flour until a soft dough is formed. Divide the dough into 4 equal portions, wrap each in plastic wrap, and refrigerate for several hours.

Combine all the filling ingredients and stir to mix well.

Preheat the oven to 350°F with the rack set in the center position. Line 3 heavy-duty baking sheets with aluminum foil or parchment paper. Working on a lightly sugared work surface, roll a portion of dough into a 9-inch circle. Cut the dough into 12 wedges. Coat one side of each wedge with a thin layer of the apricot preserves, then spread a generous amount of the raisin nut filling down the entire length and width of each wedge. Press the filling firmly into the dough with your fingers, then, starting with the wide end, roll the dough up and bend the ends in slightly to form a crescent.

Place the rugelach 1½ inches apart on the prepared baking sheets. Brush the tops with the milk, sprinkle with the cinnamon sugar, and bake one sheet at a time until the tops are golden brown and the filling is bubbling, 16 to 18 minutes. Cool for 15 minutes before removing to a wire rack to cool completely. Store in a tightly covered tin at room temperature or freeze.

# Chocolate Cherry Torte

**Serves 12**

**Max:** *When I was a kid I couldn't understand all the excitement over this cake. Now I could kick myself for every time I passed up a piece. This was my mother's first recipe in* The New York Times Sunday Magazine.

**Lora:** *Craig Claiborne changed my life when he generously ran this recipe. I love this cake as much now as I did back in 1982 when it appeared in the* Times. *Hungarian sour cherries are not always easy to find—look in gourmet shops and ethnic food stores. When I find some I always buy extra just to have them on hand. Make sure to check each one—"pitted" in Hungarian means "we left some in just to test your teeth."*

¾ cup (1½ sticks) unsalted butter at room temperature

⅔ cup granulated sugar

3 extra-large eggs

1½ teaspoons vanilla extract

½ teaspoon almond extract

8 ounces bittersweet chocolate, melted and slightly cooled

½ cup finely ground almonds

⅔ cup all-purpose flour, sifted before measuring

One 24-ounce jar sour pitted cherries in syrup, drained

2 tablespoons confectioners' sugar

8 ounces almond paste

## For the glaze

½ cup heavy cream

8 ounces bittersweet chocolate, chopped

Preheat the oven to 350°F, with the rack set in the center position. Butter a 9-inch cake pan, cover the bottom with a circle of parchment paper or waxed paper, butter the paper, and then dust the pan with flour, knocking out the excess. Either by hand or in an electric mixer, cream the butter and the sugar together until light and fluffy. Add the eggs and mix well. Mix in the extracts. Add the chocolate, nuts, and flour, mixing only until incorporated. Pour and scrape the batter into the prepared pan. Sprinkle the cherries over the top, then use your fingers to poke them into the batter so that just the very tops are showing. Bake the torte for 45 minutes or until the top looks dry but a cake tester inserted in the center shows the interior to be moist. Allow the cake to cool for 10 minutes in the pan, then invert on a rack to cool completely, bottom side up.

Place a length of waxed paper on the work surface. Sprinkle with the confectioners' sugar. Work the almond paste into a flat, round cake and place it on the paper. Cover with a second piece of waxed paper, then roll the almond paste into a 9-inch circle, using the cake pan as a guide. Remove the top piece of waxed paper and, using the cake pan as a guide, trim the almond paste into a neat circle. Invert the almond paste onto the top (actually, the smooth bottom) of the cake and peel off the remaining waxed paper. Place the cake on a serving plate and position four long strips of waxed paper under the outermost edges of the cake.

Heat the cream in a small saucepan set over high heat. When the cream just starts to simmer, remove the pan from the heat and add the chocolate. Stir gently with a wire whisk until the mixture is smooth. Pour the glaze over the top of the cake and use a long metal spatula to spread it smoothly over the top and sides. Allow the glaze to harden at room temperature for about 30 minutes before slicing.

# Index

**A**

ancho chiles, in mole truffle torte, 112–113
anchovy fillets:
  in big fish, little fish, 62–63
  in mozzarella en carrozza, 34
  and olive-stuffed potato, 108
  –stuffed olives, 26
apple(s):
  baked, stuffed with mascarpone and dried, 127
  -cranberry turnovers, 128
  in Millie's hamantaschen, 136–137
  pancake, Diane Fitzgerald's, 4
  -stuffed strudel, 129
apricot(s):
  dried, in pork loin stuffed with fruit and nuts, 96
  -filled crêpes, 132
  preserves in rugelach, 141
artichokes, sausage-stuffed, 100

**B**

bacon and blue cheese–stuffed potato, 108
banana oatmeal muffins, jumbo lemon cream–filled, 8–9
beef:
  butterflied flank steak stuffed with grainy mustard, prosciutto, and tarragon, 94–95
  fajitas, 93
  in Millie's pierogi, 35
  in Tex-Mex stuffed meat loaf, 92
biscuits, rum tums, 133

blue cheese:
  and bacon–stuffed potato, 108
  in Buffalo thighs, 31
bran muffins, stuffed, 6
bread, ricotta-stuffed garlic, 13
bread bowl:
  in honor of Jim Dodge, 23
  salmon chowder in a, 65
breakfast, Sam's best, 3
Brie, stuffed, 30
brioches, chocolate-filled, 120–121
broccoli, in whole pumpkin stuffed with curried vegetable stew, 106–107
Buffalo thighs, 31
butternut squash with curried rice and chickpea stuffing, Germaine's, 104

**C**

cabbage, green:
  filling in Louise Goldsmith's famous knishes, 32–33
  rolls, stuffed with yogurt dill sauce, 90–91
  in shrimp in tomato baskets, 72
cake:
  cassata alla Siciliana, 111
  chocolate cherry torte, 142
  chocolate cream–filled chocolate cupcakes, 118–119
  chocolate roulade filled with chocolate ice cream, 114–115
  ice cream–stuffed pound, with raspberry sauce and whipped cream, 116–117
  mole truffle torte, 112–113

calscones, 56
calzones, zucchini, summer squash, and Vidalia onion–stuffed, 54–55
cannoli, white and dark chocolate, 124
capon, roast, with oyster-cracker stuffing, 82
cassata alla Siciliana, 111
caviar, poor man's, 24
Cheddar-chile rice–stuffed tomatoes, 99
cheese, *see specific cheeses and cheese dishes*
cherry(ies), sour:
  duck breast stuffed with, 86–87
  –filled cream tart, 134–135
cherry chocolate torte, 142
chicken:
  breasts, prosciutto and Jack cheese–stuffed, 75
  Buffalo thighs, 31
  empanadas, 42
  jerk, jumbo corn muffins stuffed with, 79
  in Max's spring rolls, 37
chickpea, and rice stuffing, curried, Germaine's butternut squash with, 104
chile(s):
  ancho, in mole truffle torte, 112–113
  -Cheddar rice–stuffed tomatoes, 99
  salsa, green, 43
  serrano, in beef fajitas, 93
  *see also* jalapeño pepper(s)

chocolate:
    cassata alla Siciliana, 111
    cherry torte, 142
    chunk–filled scones, 5
    cream–filled chocolate cupcakes, 118–119
    -filled brioches, 120–121
    in ice-cream sandwiches, 122–123
    mole truffle torte, 112–113
    roulade filled with chocolate ice cream, 114–115
    in s'mores, 138–140
    white and dark, cannoli, 124
chowder, salmon, in a bread bowl, 65
cookies:
    in ice-cream sandwiches, 122–123
    Millie's hamantaschen, 136–137
    rugelach, 141
coriander, duck breast stuffed with ginger, lemon and, 84–85
cornbread, roast turkey stuffed with pecans, cranberries, and, two ways, 76–78
corned beef, in stuffed sourdough reuben, 14–15
cornish game hens, fig-stuffed, 83
corn muffins stuffed with jerk chicken, jumbo, 79
couscous, salmon stuffed with smoked salmon and, 68–69
crabmeat, in Fourth of July stuffed salmon to feed a crowd, 66–67
cranberry(ies):
    -apple turnovers, 128
    roast turkey stuffed with cornbread, pecans, and, two ways, 76–78
cream:
    –filled, chocolate, chocolate cupcakes, 118–119
    –filled banana oatmeal muffins, jumbo lemon, 8–9
    tart, sour cherry-filled, 134–135
    whipped, and raspberry sauce, ice cream–stuffed pound cake with, 116–117
crêpes, apricot-filled, 132
croissants, in Sam's best breakfast, 3
cupcakes, chocolate cream–filled chocolate, 118–119
curried:
    rice and chickpea stuffing, Germaine's butternut squash with, 104

vegetable stew, whole pumpkin stuffed with, 106–107

## D

desserts, *see specific desserts*
deviled eggs, classic, 25
dill:
    jumbo shells stuffed with feta and, in fresh tomato sauce, 48–49
    yogurt sauce, stuffed cabbage rolls with, 90–91
duck breast:
    stuffed with ginger, coriander, and lemon, 84–85
    stuffed with sour cherries, 86–87

## E

eggs, classic deviled, 25
empanadas, chicken, 42

## F

fajitas, beef, 93
feta cheese, jumbo shells stuffed with dill and, in fresh tomato sauce, 48–49
fig(s):
    in mole truffle torte, 112–113
    -stuffed cornish game hens, 83
fish:
    baked, stuffed in lettuce, 64
    big fish, little fish, 62–63
    Fourth of July stuffed salmon to feed a crowd, 66–67
    little fish, big fish, 61
    in niçoise roll-ups, 39
    salmon chowder in a bread bowl, 65
    salmon stuffed with couscous and smoked salmon, 68–69
    *see also* shellfish
flank steak, butterflied, stuffed with grainy mustard, prosciutto, and tarragon, 94–95
focaccia, plum-stuffed, 130–131
Fontina-stuffed Vidalia onions, 102
fruit, pork loin stuffed with nuts and, 96

## G

garlic:
    bread, ricotta-stuffed, 13

and olive–stuffed butterflied leg of lamb, 89
    Parmesan-stuffed potato, 108
    roasted, lamb spirals stuffed with goat cheese and, 88
ginger, duck breast stuffed with coriander, lemon and, 84–85
goat cheese:
    lamb spirals stuffed with roasted garlic and, 88
    and sun-dried tomato filling in fresh ravioli with two stuffings, 50–51
Greek salad in pita pockets, 17
green chile salsa, 43
    in chicken empanadas, 42

## H

ham, in roasted turkey with jambalaya stuffing, 80–81
hamantaschen, Millie's, 136–137
horseradish-stuffed potato, 108

## I

ice cream:
    chocolate roulade filled with chocolate, 114–115
    sandwiches, 122–123
    –stuffed pound cake with raspberry sauce and whipped cream, 116–117
Italian toast, 7

## J

jalapeño pepper(s):
    in Commander's Palace tasso-stuffed shrimp, 70–71
    stuffed with peanut butter, Sam Arnold's, 29
jambalaya stuffing, roasted turkey with, 80–81
jerk chicken, jumbo corn muffins stuffed with, 79

## K

kasha:
    filling in Louise Goldsmith's famous knishes, 32–33
    jumbo shells stuffed with, 57
knishes, Louise Goldsmith's famous, 32–33

## L

lamb:
　garlic and olive–stuffed
　　butterflied leg of, 89
　spirals stuffed with roasted garlic
　　and goat cheese, 88
　in stuffed cabbage rolls with
　　yogurt dill sauce, 90–91
lemon:
　cream–filled banana oatmeal
　　muffins, jumbo, 8–9
　duck breast stuffed with ginger,
　　coriander, and, 84–85
lentil-stuffed peppers, 101
lettuce, baked fish stuffed in, 64

## M

maki, mock, 38
manicotti, quick, stuffed with
　　spinach, pesto, and ricotta,
　　47
marinara sauce, in Italian toast, 7
mascarpone, baked apples stuffed
　　with dried apples and, 127
meat loaf, Tex-Mex stuffed, 92
mole truffle torte, 112–113
Monterey Jack cheese and
　　prosciutto–stuffed chicken
　　breasts, 75
mozzarella en carrozza, 34
Muenster and smoked turkey roll-
　　ups, 41
muffins:
　jumbo corn, stuffed with jerk
　　chicken, 79
　jumbo lemon cream–filled
　　banana oatmeal, 8–9
　stuffed bran, 6
mustard, grainy, butterflied flank
　　steak stuffed with prosciutto,
　　tarragon and, 94–95

## N

niçoise roll-ups, 39
nuts, pork loin stuffed with fruit
　　and, 96

## O

oatmeal muffins, jumbo lemon
　　cream–filled banana, 8–9
olive(s):
　anchovy-stuffed, 26

and anchovy–stuffed potato, 108
and garlic–stuffed butterflied leg
　　of lamb, 89
onion(s):
　caramelized, –stuffed potato tart,
　　105
　pearl, in whole pumpkin stuffed
　　with curried vegetable stew,
　　106–107
　Vidalia, Fontina-stuffed, 102
　Vidalia, zucchini and summer
　　squash–stuffed calzones,
　　54–55
oyster-cracker stuffing, roast capon
　　with, 82

## P

pancake, Diane Fitzgerald's apple, 4
Parmesan cheese:
　and garlic–stuffed potato, 108
　sun-dried tomatoes stuffed with
　　tapenade and, 28
pasta:
　fresh ravioli with two stuffings,
　　50–51
　jumbo shells stuffed with feta
　　and dill in fresh tomato
　　sauce, 48–49
　jumbo shells stuffed with kasha,
　　57
　quick manicotti stuffed with
　　spinach, pesto, and ricotta,
　　47
peanut butter, Sam Arnold's
　　jalapeños stuffed with, 29
pecans, roast turkey stuffed with
　　cornbread, cranberries and,
　　two ways, 76–78
peppers, lentil-stuffed, 101
pesto, quick manicotti stuffed with
　　spinach, ricotta and, 47
phyllo stuffed spinach pie, 18–19
pierogi, Millie's, 35
pita pockets, Greek salad in, 17
pizza, deep-dish stuffed, 52–53
plum-stuffed focaccia, 130–131
poor man's caviar, 24
　in bread bowl in honor of Jim
　　Dodge, 23
poppy seed filling, 137
　in Millie's hamantaschen,
　　136–137
pork:
　Commander's Palace tasso-
　　stuffed shrimp, 70–71

loin stuffed with fruit and nuts,
　　96
pot stickers, Asian, 36
sausage in roasted turkey with
　　jambalaya stuffing, 80–81
*see also* prosciutto
potato(es):
　anchovy and olive–stuffed, 108
　blue cheese and bacon–stuffed,
　　108
　filling in Louise Goldsmith's
　　famous knishes, 32–33
　garlic Parmesan–stuffed, 108
　horseradish-stuffed, 108
　in salmon chowder in a bread
　　bowl, 65
　tart, caramelized onion–stuffed,
　　105
pot stickers, Asian pork, 36
pound cake:
　in cassata alla Siciliana, 111
　ice cream–stuffed, with raspberry
　　sauce and whipped cream,
　　116–117
prosciutto:
　butterflied flank steak stuffed
　　with grainy mustard,
　　tarragon and, 94–95
　in fig-stuffed cornish game hens,
　　83
　and Jack cheese–stuffed chicken
　　breasts, 75
　in mozzarella en carrozza, 34
　in scallop roll-ups, 40
pumpkin, whole, stuffed with
　　curried vegetable stew,
　　106–107

## R

raspberry sauce and whipped
　　cream, ice cream–stuffed
　　pound cake with, 116–117
ravioli, fresh, with two stuffings,
　　50–51
reuben, stuffed sourdough,
　　14–15
rice:
　and chickpea stuffing, curried,
　　Germaine's butternut squash
　　with, 104
　–stuffed tomatoes, chile-Cheddar,
　　99
　wild, in Fourth of July stuffed
　　salmon to feed a crowd,
　　66–67

ricotta cheese:
  quick manicotti stuffed with
    spinach, pesto, and, 47
  and spinach filling in fresh ravioli
    with two stuffings, 50–51
  –stuffed garlic bread, 13
roll-ups:
  niçoise, 39
  scallop, 40
  smoked turkey and Muenster, 41
roulade, chocolate, filled with
  chocolate ice cream,
  114–115
rugelach, 141
rum tums, 133

S

salads:
  Greek, in pita pockets, 17
  shrimp in tomato baskets, 72
salmon:
  chowder in a bread bowl, 65
  Fourth of July stuffed, to feed a
    crowd, 66–67
  stuffed with couscous and
    smoked, 68–69
salsa:
  green chile, 43
  -stuffed subs, 16
sandwiches:
  Greek salad in pita pockets, 17
  ice-cream, 122–123
  Italian toast, 7
  mozzarella en carrozza, 34
  niçoise roll-ups, 39
  salsa-stuffed subs, 16
  smoked turkey and Muenster
    roll-ups, 41
  stuffed sourdough reuben, 14–15
sauces:
  fresh tomato, jumbo shells
    stuffed with feta and dill in,
    48–49
  pesto, quick manicotti stuffed
    with spinach, ricotta and, 47
  raspberry, and whipped cream,
    ice cream–stuffed pound
    cake with, 116–117
  yogurt dill, stuffed cabbage rolls
    with, 90–91
sauerkraut, in stuffed sourdough
  reuben, 14–15
sausage:
  Commander's Palace
    tasso–stuffed shrimp, 70–71

in Italian toast, 7
  pork, in roasted turkey with
    jambalaya stuffing, 80–81
  -stuffed artichokes, 100
scallop roll-ups, 40
scones, chocolate chunk–filled, 5
serrano chiles, in beef fajitas, 93
shellfish:
  Commander's Palace tasso-
    stuffed shrimp, 70–71
  in Fourth of July stuffed salmon
    to feed a crowd, 66–67
  in little fish, big fish, 61
  in mock maki, 38
  scallop roll-ups, 40
  shrimp in tomato baskets, 72
  in stuffed snow peas, 27
shells, jumbo:
  stuffed with feta and dill in fresh
    tomato sauce, 48–49
  stuffed with kasha, 57
shrimp:
  Commander's Palace tasso-
    stuffed, 70–71
  in little fish, big fish, 61
  in stuffed snow peas, 27
  in tomato baskets, 72
snow peas, stuffed, 27
sourdough reuben, stuffed, 14–15
spinach:
  in calscones, 56
  in Greek salad in pita pockets,
    17
  pie, phyllo stuffed, 18–19
  quick manicotti stuffed with
    pesto, ricotta and, 47
  and ricotta filling in fresh ravioli
    with two stuffings, 50–51
spring rolls, Max's, 37
stew, curried vegetable, whole
  pumpkin stuffed with,
  106–107
strudel, apple-stuffed, 129
subs, salsa-stuffed, 16
summer squash, zucchini and
  Vidalia onion–stuffed
  calzones, 54–55

T

tapenade, sun-dried tomatoes
  stuffed with Parmesan and,
  28
tarragon, butterflied flank steak
  stuffed with grainy mustard,
  prosciutto, and, 94–95

tart:
  caramelized onion–stuffed
    potato, 105
  sour cherry–filled cream,
    134–135
  tasso-stuffed shrimp, Commander's
    Palace, 70–71
Tex-Mex stuffed meat loaf, 92
toast, Italian, 7
tomato(es):
  baskets, shrimp in, 72
  chile-Cheddar rice–stuffed, 99
  sauce, fresh, jumbo shells stuffed
    with feta and dill in, 48–49
tomato(es), sun-dried:
  and goat-cheese filling in fresh
    ravioli with two stuffings,
    50–51
  stuffed with tapenade and
    Parmesan, 28
torte:
  chocolate cherry, 142
  mole truffle, 112–113
trout, in big fish, little fish, 62–63
truffle torte, mole, 112–113
tuna, in niçoise roll-ups, 39
turkey:
  in deep-dish stuffed pizza,
    52–53
  roast, stuffed with cornbread,
    pecans, and cranberries two
    ways, 76–78
  roasted, with jambalaya stuffing,
    80–81
  smoked, and Muenster roll-ups,
    41
turnovers, cranberry-apple, 128

V

vegetable(s), 97–108
  stew, curried, whole pumpkin
    stuffed with, 106–107

Y

yogurt dill sauce, stuffed cabbage
  rolls with, 90–91

Z

zucchini:
  baked stuffed, 103
  summer squash and Vidalia
    onion–stuffed calzones,
    54–55